OATH KEEPERS
Diminishing the Role of the Political Salesman

Dr. Cristina Guarneri

Prologue

Throughout modern American history, elected officials have sworn oaths to uphold constitutions and said the Pledge of Allegiance without much controversy. In a handful of cases recently, these routine practices have fallen victim to the same political divisions that have left the country deeply polarized.

However, unlike the Pledge of Allegiance, elected officials' ability to decline to take an oath of office often carries a higher price of being unable to hold an elected position. Even with oaths of office, for more than a century, politics has been embracing an important distinction that has been borrowed from business expertise, that selling would reach voters. It's a political salesmanship that is far more complex, a subtle art that may be the skill that politicians want to master if they're looking to have voters and to buy into what candidates have on offer.

Politics has long been intermingling with the world of commerce, from door-to-door sales to "branding" to slick advertising campaigns. The same pollsters who track the parties' fortunes also conduct consumer surveys for their corporate clients, sometimes in the same polling sample. When a politician connects with the voters, we call him or her a good "retail politician." It's not magic, and its detractors say that treating politics as a blunt, consumer-marketing exercise could even feed voter cynicism about politics.

For anyone trying to understand the nature of political campaigning in this day and age, to understand how the lessons of business marketing are increasingly being applied to the transactional relationship between politicians and voters. While we're paying attention to the ad wars between opposing political parties, in other words, perhaps we ought to be looking more closely at the marketing battle for the votes.

With this in mind, a growing academic study of the business of political marketing is giving us a whole new way of classifying what our politicians are presenting for the voters to "buy." In this world, you can be a "product-oriented party," "sales-oriented party" and "marketing-oriented party," and they come to the study of politics. Here's how the model, as applied to politics, works. In commerce, organizations can be considered to have a product, sales, or marketing orientation; that is, a philosophical approach to how to attract customers to what the business has to offer.

Motor vehicles are a common business example. Henry Ford's Model T was so revolutionary in the early decades of the 20th century that consumers bought the car even though it came only in black; the demand was such that the product sold itself into a product orientation. Over time, to stimulate sales, car companies heavily promoted their products, sometimes with hyperbolic claims or a sales orientation. As competition intensified, successful managers changed their offerings in response to consumers' preferences. From muscle cars to hybrids, today people have a wide choice of vehicles that are designed to meet their preferences, rewarding the companies best able to do so.

Political parties can have product, sales, or marketing orientations, each a more sophisticated operation than the other. A party that is product-oriented, a POP, does little more than offer itself up to electors. It exists to attract people who share a similar ideology. Such an organization does minimal self-promotion and relies on like-minded people, even candidates, seeking it out.

Gradually, politics has been embracing an important distinction, also borrowed from business expertise that selling is not the same as marketing. It's marketing, a far more complex, subtle art, that may be the skill that political candidates want to master if they're looking to have voters buy what they have on offer, a Sales-Oriented Party in politics.

Sales-oriented parties are considerably more structured and use a mix of promotional activities to communicate what they have to offer. Their fundraising machinery finances personnel, a leader's tour, signage, and advertising. Such parties have a network of salespersons knocking on doors and phoning electors to identify supporters. They emphasize media relations, use direct appeals such as targeted mailings, and embrace the latest in communications technology. They hope to stimulate demand for a somewhat ideological product.

From time to time using a Sales-Oriented Party approach usually coincides with success in opinion polls and mainstream political organizations become marketing-oriented parties. As with a sales operation, an improved return on investment is achieved by selecting promotional activities that match targeted electors' media usage. What's different is that the political product is malleable. A Marketing-Oriented Party responds to the median voter's preferences by demonstrating ideological flexibility and, if necessary, a willingness to change leadership. It communicates ideas and an overall package that research has demonstrated is likely to have broad support. The result is an efficient appeal to the largest number of possible supporters.

Parties have been responding to scientific opinion research since the Second World War, and sometimes basic political intuition can lead to success, so it's important not to overstate the model. There are so many competing interests across party lines that, to form the government, in modern times it isn't good enough to be ideological. To move into a party leader needs to lead a party that is responsive to what the electorate wants, especially if that means internal change. Monitoring opinion polls and message spin is one thing; getting the party executive and rank and file to move with the political winds is another.

It's well known that the electoral system rewards ideological parties that are regionally based, but that it discriminates against ideological national parties. What is trying to be accomplished is a model that can help us distinguish which credible national parties are fluctuating between being government contenders and pretenders. This is done by creating a product, such as a candidate, and offering a platform that would strike a balance between the interests of specific segments of the voting public, and the interests of internal party supporters." In other words, there is a power between a Sales-Oriented Party and a Marketing-Oriented Party, using marketing to sell an ideologically based product. The strategy is to avoid giving the public what it didn't want, rather than a pure effort to design a party around consumer demand.

By running a sophisticated sales operation during election campaigns, by using a platform that identifies the strengths and weaknesses of the party leaders, and informing their strategic communications decisions. They then can successfully exploit the opposing parties' weaknesses on questions of leadership and policy. Though they increased their share of seats, a sales-oriented party might arguably form a majority government.

Election campaigns are a consumer transaction. There is little room or place for vision, ideology, and principle in a political party that organizes itself around the whims of the electorate. Instead, it's a marketing orientation that encourages a bland, but pragmatic, managerial style of governance that prioritizes short-term populist decisions. What's more, consumer choices are not the same as citizen choices, and ultimately the only opportunity to "buy" a political product occurs in a one-day-only sale known as Election Day.

What is electorally important, furthermore, is whether a personable party leader can maintain the support of the party faithful as the leader shifts the organization ideologically toward the median voter. Having a marketing orientation cannot guarantee winning an election fundraising, the electoral system, regionalism, unexpected events, and so on, are just some of the challenges, but, in theory, a willingness to change in response to elector preferences should improve a party's chances. Since it is often easier to be responsive when in opposition, sustaining positive brand attributes while in power is greatly facilitated by destabilized, underfunded, and unorganized competitors. Differentiating oneself from others can involve using different strategies to weaken the brand values of opponents and to produce a product that has a more popular appeal to voters. However, in the end, it's not able seeing who can make the most promises, but rather who can keep them.

Part I

Chapter One

I Do Solemnly Swear

I, do solemnly swear that I will uphold the Constitution of the United States and the Constitution of the State of New Jersey and that I will bear true faith and allegiance to the same and the Governments established in the United States and in this State, under the authority of the people and that I will faithfully, impartially and justly perform all of the duties of the office according to the best of my ability. So help me God.

These are the words often heard when taking oath in public office, but they aren't just words, they are the promise that many people believe will be kept. For many who make this solemn vow, the promise to serve others is there. However, the longer that an elected official stays in office, the oath looks more a formality, but not all public servants will view their oath in such a way. Instead, some still hold themselves to a high standard and keep themselves accountable to the words, I solemnly swear.

Within government, individuals taking public office within the United States take an oath of office. The reason for taking such an oath is because public servants are just that, servants of the people. After much debate about an Oath, the framers of the U. S. Constitution included the requirement to take an Oath of Office in the Constitution itself. Article VI of the Constitution says "The Senators and Representatives before mentioned, and the Members of the several State Legislatures, and all executive and judicial Officers, both of the United States and of the several States, shall be bound by Oath or Affirmation, to support this Constitution; but no religious Test shall ever be required as a Qualification to any Office or public Trust under the United States." The Constitution does not prescribe the actual text of the Article VI oaths. For federal civil service employees, the oath is set forth by law in 5 U.S. Code § 3331, which reads as follows:

> "An individual, except the President, elected or appointed to an office of honor or profit in the civil service or uniformed services, shall take the following oath: "I, ___, do solemnly swear (or affirm) that I will support and defend the Constitution of the United States against all enemies, foreign and domestic; that I will bear true faith and allegiance to the same; that I take this obligation freely, without any mental reservation or purpose of evasion; and that I will well and faithfully discharge the duties of the office on which I am about to enter. So help me God."

The President is also required by the Constitution to take an Oath of Office. Article 2, Section 1, of the US Constitution prescribes the Oath. It says "I do solemnly swear (or affirm) that I will faithfully execute the Office of President of the United States, and will to the best of my ability, preserve, protect and defend the Constitution of the United States."

The Oaths are relatively straightforward, but what do they mean?

I see the oath as having three important aspects. First, the employee swears to support and defend the Constitution against enemies. Second, s/he swears allegiance to the Constitution. Finally, the employee promises to do his/her job well.

Federal workers often hear a career supervisor or political appointee talking about loyalty to the agency or the boss. One purpose of the Oath of Office is to remind federal workers that they do not swear allegiance to a supervisor, an agency, a political appointee, or even to the President. The oath is to support and defend the U.S. Constitution and faithfully execute your duties. The intent is to protect the public from a government that might fall victim to political whims and to provide a North Star — the Constitution — as a source of direction. Other laws have been enacted that support that view. For example, in 1939, Congress passed and President Franklin D. Roosevelt signed the Hatch Act. We call it that today, but the actual name of the law is "An Act to Prevent Pernicious Political Activities."

The Oath does not remove ambiguity and it is not always easy for an employee to know what to do. Here are a few examples:

- Lawful orders. Let's say someone in authority gives a federal worker a lawful order that s/he does not agree with. That disagreement might be for ethical reasons, differences in policy direction, or other reasons. Federal employees are required to follow lawful orders, even if they disagree with them.
- Unlawful orders. 5 USC 2302(b) (9) (D) gives employees the right to refuse unlawful orders. Refusing an unlawful order is not easy. The employee may face significant pressure to carry out an order that s/he knows is unlawful. Most employees never have the experience of being given an unlawful order.
- Regulatory violations. What happens when an order violates a regulation or rule, but is not technically illegal? A 2015 Merit Systems Protection Board decision answered that question. MSPB outlined the

issues in the case, writing "Specifically, the appellant asserted that the agency violated 5 U.S.C. § 2302(b) (9) (D), which protects employees from retaliation "for refusing to obey an order that would require the individual to violate a law." 5 U.S.C. §2302(b) (9) (D). He alleged that the agency improperly stripped him of particular job duties and gave him a subpar performance rating for disobeying an order that would have required that he violate (1) a Federal Acquisition Regulation that limits the authority of a contracting officer's representative (COR), and (2) "PA296: How to be a COR," the agency's training course for COR certification, which further clarifies the limitations to this authority."

- Other situations. The oath of office and most case law do not grant any protection for deciding that an order is a bad idea, bad policy, or morally wrong. In fact, the oath does not grant any protection from anything. It is an oath of allegiance and a promise to do good work. Employees who believe they are being ordered to act in a manner inconsistent with their oath of office may pursue other options, such as whistleblower complaints, contacting their Senators or Representatives or their organization's Inspector General, or any other avenue provided by law or regulation. Disobeying direct orders is generally not one of the available options. That means an employee who wants to argue that s/he is adhering to the oath of office by disobeying orders has a very tough hill to climb. There is also the option of going to the press, but that can bring its own set of risks. It is up to individual employees to decide how much risk they are willing to assume.

Federal workers are accountable to the people. Whether an employee was a supporter of one candidate or another, or doesn't vote at all is not relevant to the oath of allegiance to the Constitution. Nor is it relevant to the promise to do a good job. Most federal employees are highly professional. They understand their oath of office and take it seriously. Even though many political appointees in every Administration do not recognize the professionalism of federal workers on the day they take their own oath of office, as their experience with federal workers increases, in previous Administrations they have come to recognize the vital role federal employees play. Those serving in public office are required to carry out their oath to support and defend the Constitution. That is what most of the American people expect and deserve from their public servants.

Taking the oath as a public servant expresses a specific intention to others that a person will act truthfully. An oath is a way of promising and are often done in the name of a deity-just like swearing "under God." I, do solemnly swear aren't just words, but they are words that have a vital role in maintaining trust, integrity, and accountability to those serving the people. This includes the elements of voting and the use of ballots during the election process.

Chapter Two

The Role Of The Ballot

Primaries, such as the presidential, are one of the most important elements of the American constitutional order. Given those general elections give voters just two starkly opposed choices, it's largely through the primaries that nuance enters the political process. Parties define themselves by whom they select to run for president, and the ideological alignments that result end up defining the contours of political conflict. Yet, despite primaries' central role, nothing about them is laid out in the Constitution. The framers didn't envision American politics taking the form of two-party competition, so they gave no thought to how parties would select their candidates. This, in turn, is part of what makes the primaries so fascinating. While the Constitution itself is incredibly difficult to change, party nominating rules and state laws are much more flexible. Consequently, the presidential nomination process is one of the elements of the American political system that's changed the most — and often in ways that aren't anticipated by the people driving the change. This is what leads primaries to be so fascinating: They are genuinely unpredictable. Conceivably almost anything could happen. Although, early nomination contests didn't involve primaries.

Intraparty disputes over who should be nominated for the

presidency are as old as the republic itself. But the modern system of determining nominees through a series of state primary elections is essentially an innovation of the 1970s. Before that, parties deployed a wide range of methods. The Democratic-Republicans, the dominant political party of the early 19th century, used to select candidates via a vote of the party's members in Congress. That method let it control the White House for 20 years and lasted until the rivalry between John Quincy Adams and Andrew Jackson made the party splinter into the Democrats and the Whigs in the aftermath of the 1824 election.

Back in 1836, in the early days of Whig versus Democrat competition, the Whig Party even tried nominating several candidates simultaneously in their bid to block Martin Van Buren from succeeding Jackson in the White House. In most Northern states, William Henry Harrison appeared on the general election ballot, while Hugh White got the nod in most Southern ones. And Massachusetts Whigs went with Daniel Webster who was dominant in the state, while Willie Magnum was nominated in South Carolina. The idea was that running multiple candidates with distinct regional appeals could successfully deny Martin Van Buren a majority in the Electoral College, throwing the choice to the US House of Representatives. The selection of the Whig on each state's ballot was left up to the local party. Had the gambit worked, one could imagine the system of multiple nominees becoming entrenched, but it did not work. Van Buren won the election, and in subsequent contests the Whigs emulated the Democrats, picking a single nominee at a broad national convention with representatives from all states.

Conventions are still held today, but they are essentially publicity stunts. At best, they're counting exercises in which the point is simply to crown the candidate who already enjoys the support of most of the delegates, but historical conventions were real decision-making bodies, where a cast of locally selected elites would come together to genuinely choose someone. That opened the door to outcomes like the Whigs drafting celebrity war heroes Zachary Taylor and Winfield Scott in 1848 and 1852, without the candidates needing to mount vigorous primary campaigns.

The convention system also allowed for the emergence of "dark horse" candidates such as James K. Polk, who was the Democrat nominee in 1844. Polk was considered a contender at the start of the process. He emerged on the convention floor as a broadly acceptable second choice after various factions were deadlocked.

Conventions generally had delegates take a series of votes to winnow the field. At the 1860 Republican convention, for example, William Seward received by far the largest number of votes on the first ballot, with Abraham Lincoln finishing a rather distant second. Seward's problem, however, was that virtually all of the delegates who weren't for him were strongly against him on electability grounds, as governor of New York he had not only opposed slavery, but also signed laws advancing the rights of free black residents of the state, radical moves that much of the party thought went too far for the swing states of the Midwest. Lincoln's result gave him enormous momentum. On the second ballot, he trailed Seward by just three votes. And at that point, it just took a little more cajoling for Lincoln to get over the top. This is the beginning of when presidential primaries became more decisive.

The Progressive Era at the beginning of the 20th century saw a backlash against local party machines and their bosses dominating American politics. This backlash was especially pronounced in Western states, where reformers implemented ideas like legislating via ballot initiative at the polls. Progressive reformers also invented the presidential primary. In 1910, Oregon became the first to use a popular election to pick its delegates for national conventions, with the delegates pledged to support specific candidates. But these primaries lacked the efficacy and decisiveness of those we have today, in part because most states didn't have them and in part because the ultimate nomination decision was still made via a multi-ballot process at a national convention.

In 1912, ex-President Theodore Roosevelt decided to challenge his successor William Howard Taft for the GOP nomination. He crushed Taft in the primaries, carrying nine of the 12 states that held primaries, while Robert La Follette won two and Taft just one. But that still left 36 other states, which mostly sent pro-Taft delegates to the convention, securing him the nomination. And that led Roosevelt to bolt the party and launch an independent bid for the general election. That year's Democratic convention, meanwhile, required 24 rounds of balloting for Woodrow Wilson to prevail over the now-forgotten House Speaker Champ Clark. That meant that delegates' initial pledges to specific candidates were long irrelevant by the time the final decision to nominate Wilson was made for election. It took twelve years for primary voters to find their preferences overridden when in 1924 William McAdoo swept the Democratic primaries (largely held in the South and West) with the strong support of the Ku Klux Klan. But for precisely that reason, he was unacceptable to the party establishment back East, whose machines relied on the loyalty of Catholic voters. However, while McAdoo didn't have enough support to win, he did have enough to block the party bosses' favorite, New York Gov. Al Smith, a Catholic.

The history of primaries also shows its importance for being like beauty contests. When primaries did play a substantive role, it was instead through their function as beauty contests. Winning the 1952 New Hampshire primary let Dwight Eisenhower prove that rank-and-file Republicans, and not just party bosses, were more interested in picking a winner than in picking an orthodox conservative — thus giving the establishment permission to do what it wanted and go with Ike. However, by the same token, winning the West Virginia primary in 1960 was a way for John Kennedy to demonstrate to party leaders that a Catholic could win votes in the South. Shows how both of these examples were making a point to persuade party leaders, not a way to override their preferences. The fundamental inefficacy of the primaries was driven home by the bitter 1968 Democratic nomination contest that ultimately went to Vice President Hubert Humphrey, who didn't even enter any primary elections. However, the tumultuous, riot-scarred convention where it happened, followed by electoral defeat at the hands of Richard Nixon, spurred massive change.

After the late 1960s, the Democratic National Committee created a commission charged with proposing reforms to the nominating process. Its report brought state delegate allocations into line with the distribution of population and required state parties to adopt open procedures for selecting delegates rather than allowing state party leaders to pick them in secret. In practice, states mostly implemented this by adopting presidential primaries — which generally induced Republicans to make the same change. The new system kicked off a chaotic era in which mavericks and factional leaders could win over the objections of party leaders.

In 1972, McGovern took advantage of his reforms to win the Democratic nomination, even with an ideology so unacceptable to major party factions that the AFL-CIO didn't support him over Richard Nixon. Then in 1976, Jimmy Carter won the Democratic nomination despite a total lack of ties to the party establishment in Washington, and proceeded to win the White House and then not pursue the party's agenda. In 1976, incumbent President Gerald Ford faced an extremely strong primary challenge from conservative leader Ronald Reagan and was forced to drop the incumbent vice president from the ticket to appease conservatives. Four years later, incumbent President Carter was challenged from the left by Ted Kennedy, his re-nomination secured only by the rally-round-the-flag effect induced by the Iranian hostage crisis.

At around this time, it became in style to observe that American political parties were in decline. University of California Irvine political scientist Martin Wattenberg achieved the apogee of this literature with his 1985 classic entitled, The Decline of Political Parties in America, which cited the influence of party professionals, the rise of single-issue pressure groups, and an attendant fall in voter turnout, but also gave the elites in politics still mattered in primaries.

Over the past 35 years, incumbent presidents have had zero problems obtaining re-nomination, presidents like George H.W. Bush and Bill Clinton alienated substantial segments of the party base with ideological heterodoxy during their first term. Reagan and Clinton both passed the baton to their vice presidents without much trouble. Insurgent candidates who caught fire with campaigns explicitly promising to shake up the party establishment — Gary Hart in 1984, Pat Robertson in 1988, Jerry Brown in 1992, Pat Buchanan in 1996, John McCain and Bill Bradley in 2000, Howard Dean in 2004, Mike Huckabee in 2008, and Rick Santorum in 2012 had repeatedly gained headlines and even won state primaries. While the 1970s insurgents were able to use early wins to build momentum, post-Reagan insurgents were ground down by the sheer duration and expansiveness of primary campaigns. Political candidates used tactics that worked in relatively low-population, cheap states like Iowa and New Hampshire simply couldn't scale without access to the broad networks of donors, campaign staff, and policy experts that establishment-backed candidates. If one candidate was the clear winner in pre-Iowa endorsements and also won the nomination, then it could be said that the party had decided, and that's just what they found. In eight of 10 competitive presidential primary contests between 1980 and 2004, endorsements showed that party insiders clearly backed one candidate before Iowa, and that candidate then went on to win the nomination.

Even after winning the nomination, the work of winning office continues with momentum. With elections drawing so much attention, this may include voters needing to choose candidates that they are less familiar with on the ballot. What is fascinating is that despite not knowing who a candidate may or may not be, the order of the candidates has more significance on who will win an election. The relationship between ballot position and electoral success, AKA "name-order effects," has a long history.

In the dark ages of American politics, candidates were not beneath changing their names when listings were alphabetical, but in our enlightened times, they are more likely to sue over name order. Political candidates would change their names just to get listed first on a ballot since it was the most favorable advantage in elections. However, this advantage did not hold when voters had high recognition of candidate names. This suggests that presidential elections, where there is generally much higher name recognition than in primary and off-year elections, are less likely to be influenced by name-order effects. The flip side of this was that in this study, low name recognition meant that voters were less likely to make any choice at all for those unknown candidates. Yet, being listed first on the ballot does show greater promise in being elected by at least five percentage points. The appeal comes from choosing the first name that appeals to the voter since he or she reads down the ballot and does not fully account for the result. The presentation, also known as framing effects, can influence a person's choice in such situations as the order of products shown to online shoppers and the precise placement of items in supermarkets.

In states such as California, a unique method of assigning ballot positions is used to ensure that candidates whose surnames start with the letter "A" do not dominate the top of the ballot. After the California local election entry deadline has passed, the California Secretary of State draws a random order of the alphabet according to which candidates are listed on all ballots," the researchers' paper states. Because candidates' positions' on the ballot are quasi-random, the expectation was that the distribution of candidates' characteristics and the number of winners be similar for all ballot positions. When counting how many winners came from the first position and calculated the expected number from that position, and compared them using statistical analysis. In one out of ten elections, the candidate listed first won just because the candidate was listed first on the ballot.

The practice of being first on a ballot often receives a larger number of votes. For example, in 71 of 79 New York City Democratic Primary contests, candidates received a greater proportion of votes when they were listed first compared to any other position they were listed in. For 7 of the 71 contests where this was the case, the advantage of the first position exceeded the winner's margin, suggesting that the ballot position would have determined the election's outcomes if one candidate had held the top spot in all precincts. Individual states have turned to randomizing candidate names on paper ballots, whereas electronic voting machines can easily rotate names for each voter to avoid choice bias. However, even with the use of electronic voting. At the beginning of the 2020 pandemic, the use of paper ballots decreases the ability to randomize candidate names from choice bias. The use of electronic ballots affords for names to be randomized with each voter. In more important elections such as those for governors, senators, and the presidency, ballot positions may not have as much of an impact. However, being listed first would still give a candidate an advantage. A popular explanation is that voters indulge in "satisficing": they evaluate the candidates as they scroll down the ballot and choose the first one that meets their basic criteria, instead of selecting the best candidate from the entire list. Although there isn't enough research to justify this to be completely true.

Overseas authorities have already taken practical advantage of ballot orders. An example would be Russia's regional parliamentary elections in March 2007. In a supposedly random allocation of parties to ballot positions in these elections, the then-President Vladimir Putin's Unified Russia party appeared in the first ballot position in eight of the fourteen regions, a full six regions more than expected under a random allocation. This finding underscores the importance of ensuring that any policies done to mitigate order effects, like randomization or rotation, are done so in a fair manner, they conclude. Nevertheless, this shows that authentic randomizing of ballot orders can improve the fairness of elections. Understanding these fundamentals allows people to recognize how the psychology of elections works, but it also opens the doors to what is it that we look for in a candidate when we vote. This decision may oftentimes be unconscious and adds to fueling empty campaign promises, the war room of campaigning, and the campaign promise.

The history behind campaign promises shows several politicians that have been unable to keep to their pledges. Often, voters need to weigh their decisions as to the candidates that will represent them at every level of government. There are those in society that do believe that a politician will say just about anything to be elected, however, this is untrue. According to Bookings Institute, candidates do take their public statements seriously. They know that they're going to be held accountable by the media and the opposition. Often once elected, politicians look to keep the promises that are made during their campaigns.

When looking at campaign platforms, from 1944 to 1976, it was found that presidents had converted about seventy percent of their party's promises into policy. Through further studies, campaign promises from John F. Kennedy to Ronald Reagan had followed through on their pledges. Approximately sixty-six percent of these pledges were completed. Making good on more promises than those broken, Bill Clinton also made good on pledges. During his second term in office, Clinton had delivered on welfare reform, a diverse administration, a balanced budget, and increased funding for Head Start, and the Family and Medical Leave Act. However, what many people remember most aren't the promises that were made, but instead in 1992, George H.W. Bush had promised to not raise taxes during his 1988 campaign election and did just the opposite.

In 1932, Franklin D. Roosevelt had made a campaign promise that he would maintain a balanced budget and that he would cut government operations by twenty-five percent. In 1928, Herbert Hoover ran on the campaign slogan "Vote for Prosperity." Hoover predicted that he would be able to win the war over poverty. However, the following year, the nation plummeted into the Great Depression.

Over the years since the Great Depression, promises have become greater. In 2007, during the presidential campaign, Obama promised "change" for the people. Traveling from state to state, many believed through his speeches that he was qualified to lead the nation. Instead, too many times over, when lobbyists move in and the grader of the election and its festivities are gone, all of those promises soon disappear and what is left is disappointed people who often turn away from the idea of voting.

There is the intention to fulfill promises, but one issue that complicates the ability to keep such pledges is if the other half of Congress controls the vote it makes it very difficult for a politician to follow through on their promises. This is partially due to the way that a politician portrays themselves. The thinking is that a politician can direct change that is direct when, unfortunately, at best; all that they can do is provide a bargain with the hope to provide change. With the use of "I" Statements, which are one of the most powerful statements to use during a campaign, the intention leads itself to the understanding and the actual belief of the politician that they could keep such promises. However, the forces from within government command less flexibility when the people are looking for a politician who holds themselves to integrity and at the same time holds themselves to deliver.

During a May speech, McCain recognized that there were limits on his presidential authority, which detailed his plans for his first term. In his speech, he stated: "I am well aware I cannot make any of these changes alone. The powers of the presidency are rightly checked by the other branches of government, and I will not attempt to acquire powers our Founders saw fit to grant Congress." Often, the inability to keep to campaign promises is due to circumstances that could not be forecasted. Campaigning in 1940 for a third term, Roosevelt repeatedly pledged, "Your boys are not going to be sent into any foreign wars." The U.S. entered World War II immediately after Japan bombed Pearl Harbor in 1941. Likewise, before the 2000 election, candidate George W. Bush insisted during his campaign that he had no intention to use the military for nation-building. However, after September 11, 2001, his intention needed to change. In the history of United States Presidents, there has only been one politician who had kept all of his promises, James K. Polk. President Polk had made five campaign promises, which allowed for him to gain California from Mexico, to settle the Oregon dispute, to lower the tariff, to create a sub-treasury, and to not run for a second term.

Although many voters do recognize that uncertainty can exist. There is no clear way to know what may or may not lie ahead after the election. There is no certain way to predict the future. The only aspect the people can know is the personality of the politician. For McCain, people may have been basing their decision on past behavior of the Republican Party. For Obama, his thinking behind "Change" allowed him to take away any presidential ambitions at that time away from Hillary Rodham Clinton during the Democratic primary. That allowed for him to be a blank slate to the people. Meeting the expectations that he had planned out for government during his terms would ultimately become a balancing act.

The promise to build a universal healthcare system and to bring more military troops home from Iraq soon after taking office provided difficulties to accomplish in its entirety. In comparison to Obama's healthcare plan, McCain would have also needed to rely on tax credit for people to choose options. He vowed on the War in Iraq to never surrender. Other promises made were to stop the spending in Washington and vetoing any spending bills, while balancing a budget and combating global warming by the end of his first term in office.

Both candidates during the 2008 presidential campaign had promised to diminish lobbyists' influence and make transparency and accountability central to their administrations. However, there are ramifications to revenue in the areas of health care, education, and foreign policy. Tailoring such promises causes a block to occur in voting. With each promise, the wording is everything. A pledge to tackle a topic could be satisfied with a speech. While even the most specific vows can sometimes go unfulfilled without sparking a public discouragement, should a politician, a candidate be unable to keep their promises during when times are good in our nation it will not matter. However, if a politician, a candidate keeps their promises, but they don't work, it will matter with great importance.

Throughout all of the political legacies defined, the idea of keeping or breaking promises also does depend on how good a leader will be in office. What does get a negative view is a politician who flip-flops in office. What is also important is how honest is that politician or candidate. What's interesting about the importance of these qualities is that although the politicians have changed, the qualities that we look forward to being different haven't changed much since the war room of 1860.

Chapter Three

Campaign Messages

Campaigning is a way for politicians to influence the decision-making of the people, with a message that candidates want to share with voters. In many elections, the opposition party will try to get the candidate's "off message" by bringing up policy or personal questions that are not related to the talking points. Most campaigns prefer to keep the message broad to attract the most potential voters. A message that is too narrow can alienate voters or slow the candidate down by explaining details. One example is John McCain's campaign "Country First" which focused on patriotism. Barak Obama used a different approach by using a one-word campaign message "Change," where he ran on a consistent and simple message of "change" throughout his 2008 campaign. However, even if the message is crafted carefully, it does not assure the candidate a victory at the polls. For a winning candidate, the message is refined and then becomes theirs while in office. Even with some of the best campaigns, there are other aspects to consider; ethics and timing in a modern-day campaign.

Modern political campaigns have set new standards for how successful campaigns are conducted day-to-day. The campaign is conducted in what is seen by the public as a strict chain of command with zero tolerance for certain prohibited actions and an extended daily schedule that starts early and ends much later than most positions found in the job market; along with ethics that is to be followed. There are prohibited actions that include, but are not limited to: lying about numbers generated (i.e. phone calls that are made, doors knocked, volunteers recruited). As campaigns become more sophisticated through technology, ethics becomes an increasing issue in offices that are wirelessly connected. This is due to less direct oversight that goes outside of the chain of command, for example, asking an acquaintance for special favors or to report information), and getting non-press members talking to the press; and blogging.

Other concerns are the daily schedule of a political campaign, which often has no definite beginning or end. Instead, it is a series of tasks to be completed by certain benchmark times, otherwise often called the COB or Close of Business. COB for political campaigns is generally defined as the time at night at which it is required to report their numbers. Number reporting is generally the last action that a political campaigner takes before the Close of Business.

The role of the traditional campaign doesn't stop there. Once all the paperwork is completed, the emails have been sent, the friend calls are done, and they do other things which are not effective to do during business hours or "voter contact time." Political campaigns are generally about contacting voters and volunteers at the nuts-and-bolts level. It is dependent on state law and the preferences of campaign organizers and volunteers, a certain block of time that often ends between 8 or 9 at night. A block of time set each night is known as "voter/volunteer contact." A violation of this block of time to conduct other activities often cannot happen. A strong justification, such as attending an important meeting becomes a priority. Only a very small fraction of campaign workers do the bulk of their work during their traditional business hours and so there are steps to building a campaign.

The steps to building a campaign include not only building a campaign team that can be as small as a few people or as large as one of many people but also building a campaign plan. A campaign plan is a plan to achieve an objective, usually of a large scale over an extended period of time. It usually coordinates many activities and uses of resources involving multiple organizations. A campaign plan could also have subordinate objectives or intermediate milestones and is often broken down into phases. They often begin with an assessment of the situation to put the plan in context. Campaign plans are often created in both business and political campaigns. The plan takes into account the goal of the campaign, the message, target audience, and what resources are available. The campaign will typically seek to identify supporters at the same time as getting its message across.

A candidate needs to consider also how to communicate their campaign message, how to recruit volunteers; along a strategy for raining money. Campaign advertising draws on techniques from commercial advertising and propaganda. The avenues that are available to political campaigns when distributing their messages are limited by the law, available resources, and the imagination of the campaigns' participants. Even though the building blocks of a campaign haven't changed much over the years, the way that candidates are reaching people has changed significantly.

Social Media	Traditional Media
Two-way conversation	One-way conversation
Open system	Closed system
Transparent	Opaque
One-on-one marketing	Mass marketing
About you	About ME
Brand and User-generated Content	Professional content
Authentic content	Polished content
FREE platform	Paid platform
Metric: Engagement	Metric: Reach/ frequency
Actors: Users/ Influencers	Actors/ Celebrities
Community decision-making	Economic decision-making
Unstructured communication	Controlled communication
Real-time creation	Pre-produced/ scheduled
Bottom-up strategy	Top-down strategy
Informal language	Formal language
	Passive involvement

| Active involvement | |

* From Hausman, (2012). Major Differences between Social Media and Traditional Media.

With technology growing as a preferred means of communication through text messages, Twitter, and Facebook; media rather than traditional campaigns have become an effective way of reaching voters. The use of media marketing in political campaigns is quickly becoming the preferred method on a campaign trail. Something as simple as "likes" increases word of mouth.

During the 2012 U.S. presidential election campaigns, Mitt Romney learned the benefits of how to use social media with traditional advertising and news media outreach during his presidential election. Governor Romney experienced the power of media and how it could profoundly shift public opinion. Within the political arena, corporate communications can be used in campaigns, but the challenge became how to integrate social media with traditional media. A social media loop is developed when starting a campaign. The loop typically began with an advertising campaign designed to stimulate social media activity. If the social media conversations reached a certain level, the mainstream media would pick up the story. Once that happens, the campaign can then reinforce the coverage's impact through additional advertising, press releases, and speeches and hence starting the loop becomes new.

With this integration of social and traditional media, the influence on public opinion can be profound. During the 2012 presidential campaign, President Obama gave a talk in which he used the expression: "You didn't build that." At the time of that speech, the comment had little media attention. However, a week later, Governor Romney released an advertisement through his campaign which criticized the remark as disparaging American entrepreneurship. Social media activity heated up over the following week and soon later with mainstream media. This showed how generated mainstream news media coverage the outrage the statement through social media. This type of advertising-social media-news media chain reaction directly benefited Romney and his numbers. Because of the positive effects of using social media, his campaign began to broadcast more messages, devoting a day at the Republican National Convention to the theme of social media.

The idea to use a combination of social media and traditional news coverage increases the impact of each campaign message sought by candidates. Each message has shown that public opinion progresses through a four-stage message cycle:

- **ORIGINATION**
  The creation of a message to "shock the system" and stimulate dialogue on an issue that otherwise might be ignored. Advertising, speeches, and press conferences are used to garner further attention;

- **DISPERSAL**
  The dissemination of the message by party stalwarts, undecided voters, and even opponents who discuss and debate it in social media forums. With it, analysts could measure the extent to which social media users were sharing and spreading a specific message;

- **AMPLIFICATION**
  This occurs when a message becomes sufficiently active, it attracts the attention of members of the mainstream news media, who are among the most active users of social networks. If the mainstream media starts to report on the message, the coverage intensifies and validates the theme in ways that can shape and move public opinion; and

- **REINFORCEMENT**
  Occurs once a message has been adopted by the news media, a campaign can reinforce it with additional advertising and speeches.

The ability of a campaign to influence news media is limited. Social media has changed that way of thinking. Social media provides a more powerful discussion platform than ever before, while at the same time, it can connect people to an interest in a topic, regardless of the persons' location or time of day. Campaign professionals can monitor and measure the activity and predict if and when a message will go to the mainstream media political parties can send a particular message through campaign messages and the advancement of social media if traditional news media follows within approximately a week after the message has been launched. If a message doesn't receive the anticipated participation within two weeks, it has little to no hope of gaining attention and it becomes time for a new message to be used. However, once a specific message has achieved significant momentum and exposure, it has the potential to transition into a traditional news media story and can later be reinforced by the candidate with further communication where social media can open a new window. This was seen in 1952, during Eisenhower's campaign for president.

Eisenhower received negative criticism for hiring an advertising agency to help leverage the new medium of television. By using commercials, he was able to deride the selling of the presidency as if he were a product, such as dishwashing detergent. However, since Eisenhower's campaign, times have changed. Today, companies now can learn to sell products by modeling how presidential candidates are marketed. Social media has opened a modern window through where they can watch in real-time as a story develops, how opinions are formed, and the news media takes an interest and minds change. Integrating that capability with their other communications tools can give companies; along with political parties, another significant capability to shape their stakeholders' opinions. However, at the same time, not understanding how social and traditional media work together can nullify a company's ability to spot and respond effectively to harmful messages as they build momentum and attract the interest of traditional media and grassroots approaches to government.

The ability to use a grassroots approach to governing depends on the ability of the politician to have a strong understanding of grassroots. Using a grassroots approach is not like any other way of governing in politics. A strategy that if not calculated corrected could fail. Renew America defines what is meant by grassroots as being at the bottom of the political pyramid, opposite the "establishment," which controls the top.

The Grassroots approach is not just reaching a younger generation of politicians, but to veterans as well. An example of such an approach beginning is the 2015 senate campaign. Iowa Jane Jech is proposing to return dollars and control back to the local government. Moving away from a one-size-fits-all for programming can lead to government bureaucracy. Other candidates such as Wisconsin Governor Scott Walker are proposing a grassroots approach for the 2016 campaign for president. With a commitment to transform America, and to transfer power from the nation's capital in Washington back to the states and to the cities within the United States, where the people could hold their government accountable.

The grassroots way of thinking took him to new heights in the election process. Often, candidates may be told that running a campaign solely on a grassroots initiative could be the wrong way to go. However, practicing a grassroots approach not only in theory but as a strategy may bring a candidate the polls that are desired within elections. By keeping to a Grassroots Campaigns to build support for progressive candidates, parties, and causes through engaging everyday people in political action, politicians can begin to bring awareness for a type of campaigning that made past leaders such as Abraham Lincoln well-respected. With an emphasis on small-donor fundraising, the use of a grassroots campaign helped him to change how someone who may have been seen as the average person interacts effectively with a political party. The results allow for many candidates to be able to sign on thousands of new supporters and raising millions of dollars. More importantly, for everyday people to see they could impact the political process.

When looking at the research on grassroots campaigns, in 2008, Grassroots Campaigns advocated for candidates who were running for office, helped to recruit volunteers to elect Barack Obama and other Democrats in battleground states. Many key organizations have helped to organize 7,480 house parties where volunteers made 2.14 million calls and recruited over 90,000 volunteers for Obama in swing states. Additionally, grassroots campaigns have helped to register over 230,000 new voters in 13 battleground states, which helped to win many states and turned North Carolina blue for the first time since Jimmy Carter's election in 1976. Politicians are becoming inventive and their way of thinking is bringing them to be separate from the usual politician. Candidates who hold a business background, when entering into a campaign strategy because was is being enforced is no longer the thinking that the campaign is no longer being run like a candidate would, but instead, as a business man would run a campaign for their businesses. It becomes less of a far stretch to use the experiences that are gained when working in Corporate America or the knowledge that is through business education to recognize to reach a win of votes would mean reaching the people. This is the idea of bringing forth a grassroots initiative to the political campaign and allows for a politician to mobilize a progressive movement.

Going door to door with a platform for hiring more police officers and improving parking and managing the city's rapid development, politicians can bring in the votes among the community's diverse set of voters in every socioeconomic area. A campaign that features several tactical innovations, one being not to distribute campaign signs to earn supporters. The thinking is to put together a marketing strategy for winning.

It was a grassroots marketing plan that is now being carried out within their communities. Taking advertising to the potential customer through a variety of strategies, such a campaign kept to a firm plan often very effective for businesses in all stages of development. Politicians are using their positions as a candidate for public office to becoming a newly formed business. It is a benefit for candidates to get their names out, and to establish themselves as a brand that would stay on the voter's mind. In theory, when branding -- or re-branding -- a business, grassroots marketing can quickly establish an image.

The idea of using grassroots marketing is to saturate the people with talk about their platforms. To do this effectively, there is often little to no choice, but to keep to their branding, the name in front of the people and on their minds. The message that the candidate has to send out needs to be updated often, if not, the name and the platform would then become repetitive and eventually ignored. This is what is called good business in campaigning.

It may have seemed easy, but the truth was that even though the effort of using a grassroots campaign can work to a candidate's advantage, however, there are still many among political parties that do watch to see how the process unfolds. For many potential candidates, there is help.

PART II

Chapter Four

History Repeats Itself

Civil wars are not uncommon in American history. They're not just saved for clashes between people and the government, but rather for issues such as economic, cultural, and the power of the federal government to control states. Civil wars can occur for three main reasons, conflicts, national identity divided, and a shift occurs from tribalism to sectarianism. Tribalism happens when people begin to believe that the best interests of the larger community are taken to heart. In sectarianism, we see the political, social, and economic elites that anyone who disagrees with them is bad and actively working to destroy a community. The United States displays these three main reasons, and many historians may very well identify that a Civil War is on the brink of happening. We see it in Congress, and we see it during the Coronavirus response where politics is wrecking America's response to the pandemic. Rather than the pandemic bringing a nation together, it has instead contributed to a growing political divide in the United States. Partisan affiliation is often the strongest predictor of both behavior and attitudes about the coronavirus, even more, powerful than local infection rates and demographic characters such as age and health status. Within a state partisan's organization, there is an explanation of its public health policies, including the timing and duration of stay-at-home orders, bans on social gatherings, and mask mandates.

When looking at the unfortunate implications of public health policy, the power isn't within the theory of evidence, but instead on the relative power of partisans. State leaders have missed opportunities to adopt mask ordinances, limit gatherings in the most dangerous of indoor spaces, and allow businesses to operate safely. However, bad pandemic policies have been distorted by partisanship, which has cost jobs and lives, as the downplaying of the coronavirus, as well as the opposition to mask-wearing and other precautions, have had real consequences for health and safety. But the polarization of the pandemic has had another unfortunate side effect for economic harm. Although, pandemics aren't anything new to the government.

The coronavirus outbreak continues to spread across the U.S. as a new concept that is overtaking the United States. However, looking back at the influenza pandemic of 1918 reveals that a chaotic White House response to a public-health emergency is nothing new. A political leader has spoken about the fight against coronavirus as a war against an invisible enemy, but a little over 100 years ago, President Woodrow Wilson was fighting both kinds of war: the Great War in Europe was in its final stages as the flu pandemic swept the globe, including the United States. Wilson chose to focus on the battlefronts of Europe, virtually ignoring the disease that ravaged the home front and killed about 675,000 Americans.

In terms of managing a federal response to the pandemic, there was no leadership or guidance of any kind directly from the White House. Wilson wanted the focus to remain on the war effort. Anything negative was viewed as hurting morale and would have hurt the war effort.

Shall We Wake the President: Two Centuries of Disaster Management from the Oval Office by Tevi Troy ranked Wilson as the number one worst president in a disaster. "The federal response to the influenza outbreak in 1918 can best be described as neglectful. Hundreds of thousands of Americans died without President Wilson saying anything or mobilizing nonmilitary components of the U.S. government to help the civilian population." He also faulted Wilson for contributing to the massive spread of the disease by continuing troop mobilizations even as World War I was winding to a close.

Wilson's lack of leadership on the flu did not necessarily come from any ignorance of how serious the disease was. There were reports of illness striking young, healthy soldiers in military barracks and on troop transport ships where overcrowding and poor sanitation were rampant. While Wilson never issued a public statement about the illness, Barry believes the President had many conversations about the high numbers of ill and incapacitated troops at the front. According to Alfred W. Crosby's *America's Forgotten Pandemic: The Influenza of 1918*, Wilson had asked Army Chief of Staff General Peyton March in October 1918 if he had heard of the popular jump rope rhyme parodying the virus, and recited part of it.

First Lady Edith Wilson once delivered 1,000 roses to female war workers who had come down with the Spanish flu. A niece of the President's apologized to him in a letter for failing to meet the Liberty Loan program quota due to social interactions being curbed because of influenza. Even two of the White House sheep that grazed on the front lawn were stricken but recovered, along with White House staffers who had become ill with influenza, including President Wilson, while in Paris to negotiate the Treaty of Versailles after World War I.

Pandemics impose death, often on a massive scale. Whenever a pandemic causes a major demographic collapse, it can also change relative factor prices: the economic returns to labor versus land or capital. This may lead to substantial changes in economic and political organization. It is widely acknowledged that differences in factor prices shape economic inequality, which, in turn, affects both the incidence of democracy and the quality of democratic representation.

Pandemics can also influence politics in the long run if the loss of life is high enough to increase the price of labor that is relative to other factors of production. When areas are hit the hardest, people are more likely to exhibit electoral behavior that indicates independence from mass politics to socialism, as significantly lower vote shares for Hitler's National Socialist Party in the Weimar Republic's fateful 1930 and July 1932 elections.

We can see if we look at the past that history repeats itself, and it will continue to do so. It's a constant Civil War that will plaque government and the American people, as threats to democracy and the separation of political party powers will plaque everyday living and decision-making. Much like the flu of 1918, there wasn't much expectation by the American people that government would intervene to help them, as they faced something similar to the coronavirus. Overall, Washington played a much smaller role in people's lives then as they do today, making the need to find political reformers far more necessary than a political salesman for leadership.

Often look to political leadership for help, and perhaps the answers aren't in today's leaders, but rather in those of the past. Lincoln's level-headed nature would have been a huge asset in a time that is very charged with differing opinions and passion behind those opinions. The Sixteenth President would have used what was available to liberate the people. We know this because Lincoln lived a very charged period in our nation's history, the Civil War.

Lincoln's trademark was to bring in people with differing opinions from his and try to form the best policies based on those differing viewpoints. In a time like this, Lincoln would certainly have turned to experts to guide his decision-making. Although the United States is currently in a state of transition, we could get a lot about how Lincoln might have handled going back to work and rebuilding the economy in his second inaugural address, as he was no stranger to the disease.

During his presidential term, the United States went through a deadly toll of the disease. Cholera, consumption, and typhoid claimed the lives of many Americans, including Lincoln's friends and family members. Still, as president, he never faced the kind of pandemic now spreading across the world. Lincoln was such a big people person, a stay-at-home order would have pained him so much, and Lincoln would probably have ended up with the coronavirus when he was President of the United States.

In early 1861, however, Americans faced a crisis of a different sort. It ushered in an era of unprecedented uncertainty and foreboding that threatened the lives of millions, as well as the very existence of the nation. Seven southern states seceded from the Union following the election of 1860. Many white southerners feared that President-elect Lincoln and the new Republican Party would attack slavery and, in the process, radically alter their way of life. In response, they formed a new nation, elected a president of their own, and vowed to resist any attempt by the federal government to coerce them back into the Union. However, the next four years were terrible for nearly every community, both North and South. Before it was over, the war claimed approximately 2% of the American population; should a catastrophe on such a scale befall America today, it would claim approximately 7 million people.

For the last century and a half, whenever Americans have confronted moments of vast uncertainty, they have turned to Lincoln and the example he set during the Civil War. Today's leaders might find that tradition useful. By doing so, they could see that Lincoln always pushed on despite hardships, listened to new ideas, and embraced new technology, and he could clearly state the nation's peril without suggesting the situation was hopeless.

Lincoln was a person of tremendous resilience. His early life was filled with hardship and loss, but instead of giving up or becoming embittered by the many challenges thrown his way, he always pushed forward. His path to the presidency was not an easy one, but the many adversities he was forced to endure prepared him to lead the nation through the tragedy of civil war. He lost scores of personal friends during the conflict, as well as his son Willie, but even in his grief, he remained resolute.

Our present crisis is filled with heartbreaks and setbacks, but cultivating a Lincoln-like resilience will allow us to mourn our losses while still moving forward to confront new challenges.

Another useful characteristic proved to be Lincoln's enduring interest in innovation and technology. More than a decade before being elected president, Lincoln received a patent for his invention that lifted riverboats over shoals and other obstructions. Around the same time, Lincoln began using the telegraph, and as president, he used the invention to follow the war and communicate with his generals on the front lines. Lincoln hoped new technology could bring an end to the conflict. He often met with inventors and encouraged their efforts. He even test-fired newly developed weapons on the White House lawn and made recommendations for their implementation on the battlefield.

Lincoln's habit of questioning tried-and-true methods throughout the war proved essential to his success. When his generals failed to achieve victories using traditional tactics, Lincoln borrowed books on military strategy from the Library of Congress and challenged them to adapt to changing realities. "The dogmas of the quiet past are inadequate to the stormy present," Lincoln told Congress in late 1862, as he targeted the entrenched institution of slavery. "The occasion is piled high with difficulty, and we must rise with the occasion. As our case is new, so we must think anew and act anew. We must disenthrall ourselves, and then we shall save our country," Lincoln advised.

In our current crisis, an innovative spirit from our state and national leaders, medical professionals on the front lines, and scientists working behind the scenes to develop effective treatments and a vaccine will likely be critical to our success. Perhaps Lincoln's greatest attribute during the war proved to be his ability to communicate. As president-elect, with secession threatening to derail his presidency, Lincoln could have blamed his predecessors for their failed leadership, but he did not use his platform to convey that message. Instead, he carefully articulated the challenges ahead and clearly defined why confronting and overcoming them was necessary.

To amplify his message, Lincoln sometimes wrote public letters that were printed in newspapers and composed some of the most eloquent, yet readable, speeches in American history. While his finely crafted Gettysburg Address and Second Inaugural are his most revered efforts, he rarely missed an opportunity to strengthen the nation's resolve and articulate what was at stake, which was no less than America's novel form of self-government, which Lincoln called "the last best hope of earth."

Today, we look to our leaders to emulate Lincoln's example during this time of great uncertainty. From the Great Depression and World War II to 9/11, the American people have proved that we can handle hard truths. Armed with facts and buoyed by occasional reassurances, we have also demonstrated a remarkable ability to find solutions, even in the darkest of circumstances.

Chapter Five

Leadership Lessons

In 1860, Abraham Lincoln won the presidency in 1860 and how he ended up with a cabinet filled with people he had run against in that presidential election. Lincoln looked for ways to engage with the people. Lincoln's way of leadership provides insight as to what made him to be the president that he became, but also what brought his administration to over time come to respect him. There are twenty different leadership lessons to government according to the practices of Abraham Lincoln. These practices are what lead him to become known as a 'people's president.

At the beginning of Lincoln's political career, his first goal was to win the respect of the people he knew. When he ran for representative while he still lived in Illinois, where he took became a favorite of almost everyone. This brought Lincoln to attain the admiration of everyone who had voted for him. This was enough to make his defeat seem slightly less bitter.

Lincoln never lost track of where he came from as a person. He always kept it in his head that he had gotten less than a year of formal schooling. He knew that he had never had money. He knew that he was from the frontier while other people in his political circles had grown up in full-fledged cities or otherwise established areas in the East. He knew these things, but he always fought to combat his disadvantages rather than let them beat him.

Lincoln fought melancholy with humor. When not in the company of others, he never let himself stay down for too long, and made his audience forget he had been down with his funny anecdotes and stories.

Wherever he went, Lincoln made friends. His heart and mind were always open to new people. Lincoln is renowned in history as an amazing storyteller – he was able to draw people in with these stories without making them feel like they were being hit on top of the head with a hammer. They were fully engaged with him once his stories started.

One thing that people often miss about Lincoln is that he was a genius. One of the reasons it's easy to miss this is because one of his great gifts was taking a complex concept and whittling it down so that anybody could understand it. For example, Goodwin notes that Lincoln used the following story to explain the state of slavery in the union in the 1850s: He asked his audience to imagine that there is a bed where your children are sleeping, and you see snakes in there with the children. Now, you could try to kill the snakes, but you might hurt the children, or the snakes might bite the children. Imagine, then, if there was a whole other bed where you could put your children, and you wouldn't have to deal with the snakes at all. Would you hesitate to make that decision? The open bed represented the free territories that did not yet have slaves in them. Lincoln took advice, but in the end, he always trusted his counsel most. He could gracefully accept compliments and votes of confidence without getting an ego about him.

Lincoln gained a reputation for always thinking of the bigger picture first. Early in his political career, he had a chance at winning an election in Illinois. Lincoln had forty-seven votes. Lyman Trumbull had just five votes. However, those five votes had been preventing Lincoln from getting the win, and he didn't want a door to open for the Democrats to win, so he gave his forty-seven votes to Trumbull. Many people could not believe that Lincoln had let a man with five votes win, which helped position his party.

For a man that was president during the Civil War. There

were countless instances where people around him were fighting each other or egged him on to fight someone. He stood at a distance and kept himself neutral to all parties involved.

Lincoln did not let himself get weighed down by grudges. He befriended Trumbull rather shortly after that election debacle. When he first met Edward Stanton, Stanton looked at him in contempt and proceeded to ignore him. This did not prevent Lincoln from naming Stanton his Secretary of Defense. How important are grudges in the end? Abraham Lincoln was a great student of the people. He knew how to identify strengths in others, just as he knew his strengths. He put his cabinet together, as improbable as it was, based on what each man could do.

In the 1840s, Lincoln decided his position on slavery was that it should remain untouched where it currently existed, but that it should not be allowed to spread. He, unlike most politicians, was no flip-flopper. Lincoln kept to this philosophy while shifting from the Whig party to the new Republican Party and he maintained it until he issued the Emancipation Proclamation in 1862. Had the Civil War not been as disastrous as it was, he might never have changed his position in public.

Lincoln also had enduring patience; along with an incredible sense of timing. He waited and waited for the right general, or for the wrong general to do the right thing. He waited until the right moment to announce he was running for the Presidency. He waited for the exact right moment to announce his Emancipation Proclamation to his cabinet and the world.

Being endlessly compassionate, Lincoln took to a little girl who wrote to him that her father had been killed in the war. It was Lincoln who took the time to write back to her and let her know he had also lost a parent when he was young, and how unfair it was that a child should have to go through that.

As a leader and as a person, Lincoln empathized with people easily. This allowed him to be compassionate, but it also allowed him to better understand people.
Although he stated he was a fatalist in philosophy, Lincoln worked as hard as he could at achieving the success he knew he wanted.

When news reporters came to talk to him after he was nominated, he wowed them by reciting details about every state's political situation. He worked to get nominated, he worked to get elected. He was always calculating. He just wasn't a jerk about being calculating.

Ambition is different from being a braggart. Lincoln didn't toot his own horn, but he knew that he wanted to be remembered as someone who had accomplished good things. This ambition drove him to excel from his childhood to the end of his life.

A pivotal point that often doesn't get discussed very often is that Lincoln was okay with shooting for a second. His opinion was that if people already have a "first love," you can't necessarily talk them out of it. However, if they leave that first love, he would be able to swoop in and win their hearts. This is exactly what happened at the 1860 Republican Convention. Everyone thought William H. Seward would come away with the nomination, but as rivalries stirred trouble, Lincoln remained the only person that no one had a problem with, and that's how he won.

Lastly, Lincoln knew how to engage through leadership because he went out to meet his people. He was the only candidate in 1860 to leave his hometown and travel around the country, especially around New York and New England. During the Civil War, he went to military hospitals to visit the sick and wounded. Towards the end of the war, he went down to Richmond to see the people in the defeated capital.

Lincoln as a leader brought to many, both those involved in politics and to the people that a way of governing that was sound and sincere was possible. Even though technological advancements such as social media were not available during Lincoln's time while president, he was able to reach everyone and to communicate ideas and thoughts by making the initiative to be present in the lives of the people. Lincoln had become an example of a modern-day politician by sticking to ethical principles and withstanding the bureaucracy that currently exists in government.

The potential to have ethics in government is a powerful

aspect of leadership. Very few in politics have been able to withstand bureaucracy. With having the best intentions when initially entering into office, after years of power and influence, we regrettably find government leaders losing sight of their ethics. History shows us that Founding Father George Washington needed time to know how to do the right thing. With time he became a true civil servant for the American people. However, it wasn't until 1860 that the nation had experienced ethical leadership with the electing of the sixteenth president of the United States, Abraham Lincoln.

Abraham Lincoln, otherwise nicknamed Honest Abe, was regarded as having an incredible impact on America. Even through Lincoln's law practice, this is what primarily had won him his reputation for exacting honesty. "Resolve to be honest at all events," Lincoln advised aspiring law students, "and if in your judgment you cannot be an honest lawyer, resolve to be honest without being a lawyer.

With a distinctly humane personality, Lincoln believed in the ideals that all have the opportunity to succeed. Holding to the saying: keep your friends close and your enemies closer, Lincoln built a cabinet that gave him an advantage. Throughout that Lincoln never left behind or "rose above" the role of "politician," but rather fulfilled the highest possibilities of this peculiarly honorable democratic vocation. Lincoln embraced the political life without either compromising morals at inconvenient moments or making a cipher of his politics. What he did instead, as a lifelong politician, was to realize that role's fullest moral possibilities.

With political leadership has changed since the days of Abraham Lincoln, many still wonder if such a Lincoln could exist and if it would even be possible in our political climate. The fact is– Lincoln is still with us today. The struggle for unity, freedom, war, and civil equity; Lincoln had experienced these same issues during his presidency.

What is different about today than the days of the Civil War is that Lincoln felt in all things compassion to be there for the people and to offer to understand. To be a caring citizen in times of despair and a handshake during his election years; the type of political leader that anyone could sit down with and have a cup of coffee. As a nation, we have drifted away from that type of leadership, but there is hope. With a new type of candidate that is emerging in politics that may slowly filtrate into elected offices across the nation. Something I like to call "Lincoln Leadership." Not the usual way of thinking, this new type of candidate is looking to reach people right in their neighborhoods and communities. Beyond reaching people it is also a matter of stricter measures of accountability and transparency.

Lincoln would have found the bureaucracy in government today to be discerning. This new modern-day Lincoln is slowly emerging in our nation and it is taking on the same philosophy as Lincoln did– to not make enemies when he could make friends of them. This new emerging leadership affords for those in government to reflect on their actions before taking them.

Lincoln understood the importance that his role held to meeting the needs of the American people, an insight that the younger generation of political-minded candidates is embracing. To some degree, every American claims a part of Lincoln in their life. He is always looking over us and preaching to us, forever his ghost remains with us.

With the Declaration of Independence, the Constitution, and a new type of Lincoln Leadership developing, as a country we fortunate enough that an Abraham Lincoln was in America. We continue to be fortunate that he's still with us today, as we keep Lincoln in our mind, looking back to Lincoln more than occasionally with new leadership today. We are finding that the movement towards a modern-day Lincoln may still be able to exist. Some familiar approaches, especially in campaigns have shown a new side to politics.

Campaigning, like Lincoln, to the average citizen means meeting met them where they live, by reaching out to them as they walked their children to school or for a cup of coffee at a local diner. It was about meeting people and making mental note of their needs. Politicians are laying down a framework for his campaign. Quite similar to that of Abraham Lincoln, after Lincoln's defeat in the race for the U.S. Senate, his style avoided the wordy moral rhetoric of the abolitionists in favor of clear and simple logic. Lincoln was successful in laying the groundwork for his candidacy. More importantly, Lincoln had established a solid group of campaign managers and supporters who came to the Republican convention prepared to deal, maneuver, and line up votes for Lincoln. Politicians are beginning to build a solid group of volunteers for the campaign, but it also has to do with a candidate's ability to show character on the campaign trail.

In essence, much of leadership has to do with character. According to the Josephson Institute, the approach used is based on six pillars of character. These six pillars are trustworthiness, respect, responsibility, fairness, caring, and citizenship.

A further definition of each is below.
- Trustworthiness: to be honest, be reliable, have the courage to do the right thing by building a good reputation, and being loyal;
- Respect: to treating others with respect, follow the Golden Rule, to being tolerant of differences, Use good manners, be considerate of the feelings of others, do not threaten, and deal peacefully with anger, insults, and disagreements;
- Responsibility: to do what you are supposed to do, always do your best, use self-control, be self-disciplined, think before you act, and be accountable for your choices;
- Fairness: to play by the rules, take turns and share, be open-minded; listen to others, do not take advantage of others, and do not blame others carelessly;
- Caring: to be kind, be compassionate and to showing that even in politics there is care, express gratitude, forgive others and help people in need; and
- Citizenship: to do your share to make your community better, cooperate, get involved in community affairs, stay informed, be a good neighbor, obey laws, and respect authority.

For some who may look at these and say that these characteristics of the six pillars may seem elementary and to some extent, they are in many ways, However, they are the basis in politics, looking at character and integrity are the basis of our values. These are values that are learned and practiced from a young age. However, when examining a modern-day Lincoln, it is a process of looking at the consensus of the people. Lincoln and a new breed of politicians are showing similarities to their style of campaigning. Shaking hands with the people and going door-to-door to win an election, Lincoln, who had won with an electoral victory and a substantial popular vote of fifty-five percent, up to the very eve of the election, Lincoln was doubtful about his chances of winning. It showed that Lincoln to not underestimate the intentions of the people.

In reality, however, Lincoln's chances were better than anyone guessed at that time. Lincoln's campaign slogan of "not changing horses in mid-stream" made sense to most Americans or to not change leaders during a crisis. Stability would help increase problem-solving, a philosophy that large numbers of Democrats supported. For Lincoln, it was the best hope of preserving the Union. For a new politician, it would mean to build further on the thinking that Abraham Lincoln once said, "Character is like a tree and reputation like its shadow. The shadow is what we think of it and the tree is the real thing." It is a truthful way of looking at politics, to stop and think about how this quote relates to the candidates we vote for in each election. The shadow of the people who run for office, if they are not in an as positive light as you would like, then it is probably time to look at the tree. The tree doesn't lie. It is the real thing.

Building a modern-day Lincoln includes bringing in their opponents. It would have to take work hard to instill trust in them as well. Gathering with hundreds of supporters, he planned to work relentlessly to make sure that those who had put their faith in him and his team would be made proud. Like Lincoln, politicians need to believe in this great American experiment called democracy not just through words, but in action as well.

Chapter Six

Political Branding

Branding is not a foreign or unknown strategy in politics. The idea of developing a brand, logo, and slogan to brand campaigns has been in existence as far back as 1856. Such branding brought political candidates to be recognized by voters. The "Free Soil, Free Labor, Free Speech, Free Men, Fremont" came from the U.S. presidential campaign slogan of John Fremont. In 1860, it was "Vote yourself a Farm," the U.S. presidential campaign slogan of Abraham Lincoln. "Let Us Have Peace" was the 1868 presidential campaign slogan of Ulysses S. Grant.

By 1872, the people began to see branding campaigns such as "Grant Us another Term for the presidential campaign slogan of Ulysses S. Grant. By the year 1916, the U.S. Presidential slogan for Woodrow Wilson was "He kept us out of war." In 1924, it was "Keep Cool and Keep Coolidge" — the 1924 presidential campaign slogan of Calvin Coolidge. However, it was 1932 that brought us Happy Days Are Here Again for the Democratic presidential candidate Franklin D. Roosevelt. Being Wild about Harry, led the 1948 campaign of Harry S. Truman to become President. Jimmy Carter capitalized on his heritage for peanuts with his branding of "Not Just Peanuts." As the years of political branding continued, Bill Clinton branded his campaign for "It's Time for a Change" and "Putting People First," along with Mitt Romney's 2012 branding,

"Believe in America."

Politics took on the characteristics of what many businesses were already practicing. Importance of branding is the key to success. It is the quickest way for a company to express what they have to offer. Without an effective branding campaign, it can often become difficult for people to understand why the business exists. Branding becomes important not only in name recognition, but in the consumer's ability to decide if they want to buy a product or not, how to use a service, and how they view the brand. Brand promotion and advertising may determine the consumer's ability to return. The qualities of the product or services are ensured through the customer's minds from the brand image.

A brand is a company's face to the world. It is the company's name, how that name is visually expressed through a logo, and how that name and logo are extended throughout an organization's communications. A brand is also how the company is perceived by its customers -- the associations and inherent value they place on your business. It is kind of a promise, quite similar to what is represented in political campaigns. It is a set of fundamental principles that are understood by any consumer that comes into contact with a business.

It is also an organization's reason for being and how that reason is expressed through its various communications media to its key audiences, including customers, shareholders, employees, and analysts. A brand can also describe these same attributes for a company's products, services, and initiatives.

The brand is not only convenient for businesses for repeated customer purchases, but it also becomes easier for customers to filter out the countless generic items that are out there. Branding gives consumers the reason to buy it and wastes less time for a consumer to choose. There are ways to improve a brand from advertising such as viral campaigns, which have become more trustworthy by using online ads, print ads, and commercials. Another way to improve a product or service is through reinforcing the brand. This is a good way to promoting a brand, while always being at the cutting edge or the customer's first image of a product.

The qualities of branding products and services as long as advertising is done as much as possible spreads a message and makes it into a well-recognized brand. Branding doesn't only benefit the business, but the consumer as well. The brand that a consumer chooses, often reflects who the consumer is and expresses the consumer on what they like to do and be able to join the community of like-minded consumers. Branding is a win situation for both the businesses and the loyal consumer. This way of thinking is very true when looking at the branding of politics.

For many who are new to the concept of branding in elections, branding in politics may be seen as destroying the democratic process where the obsession with an image would take away from the marketing promise and the experienced reality. However, political branding has become essential to expressing what a candidate is trying to achieve. Political branding has become an organizational principle in government.

Encompassing a marketing campaign that would be comprehensive, that would feature a new logo, tagline, and website, along with social media and taxi and subway advertisements, amongst other print, broadcast, and outdoor advertising would not be an easy task to fulfill. Although with the branding idea to bring more people into an election, political reformers use their business experience to work to their advantage. Their philosophy was that the jurisdiction, either it be a city, suburb, county, state, or nation is looking to serve should continue to attract families, young professionals, and other residents into the city. Those who are seeking to live in a diverse, metropolitan center with vibrant neighborhoods, culture, and recreational opportunities. Using a branding and marketing campaign helps political reformers to refocus the image of the community of people, as opposed to the rest of the region, the nation, and the world to expand on that growth as the geographical location would work to become the best in America.

Political reformers have the main goal to use a marketing

campaign to highlight the diversity of the city's neighborhoods and attractions throughout the area. The broad objectives of such a branding strategy were to include:

- Distinguish the area from other cities and communities, and establish its role as a regional and national leader, for example, "The Best Mid-Size City in the United States;

- Reinforce and direct focus toward the area's competitive advantages;

- Increase the area's capacity to attract real estate development and residents;

- Encourage other groups (e.g. hospitals, real estate developers, retail, small business and industry, colleges, community groups, and tourism organizations) to participate in cohesive communications and branding efforts;

- Further, enhance a sense of community; and

To promote and market the area as a premier travel destination for both the leisure and business traveler, domestically and internationally.

An example of a campaign strategy is through putting together panels to review initiatives such as contests, where submissions can be selected and interviewed about their proposals. The winning submission receives a five thousand dollar prize. Using citizen entries is one of the most comprehensive marketing plans used today. By using such an initiative, the people are given a decision-making ability unheard of that ultimately created civic pride.

Rebranding an area is a huge undertaking. This is especially true with diverse cities in the country, some candidates realize early that it isn't an easy achievement, but at the same time, they also know it could be achieved. Creating an ad campaign that reflected the diversity of the city while featuring the people who lived there, was just one way to help the city's growing real estate market.

Using a business sense above political ideas allows for campaigns to increase in awareness. Ultimately, the investment of using branding attracts and positions in a way that there was more to the candidate and its platform. Instead, it built excitement towards a new future for the people. Without more initiatives for political reformers, democracy becomes vulnerable to deteriorating. Once strong, political parties are losing their ability to maintain a balance between their principles and their brand. Not being able to hold onto a positive brand puts political parties in jeopardy of losing voter confidence. We see this beginning to occur with the Republican Party and a new textbook definition to ethics.

Chapter Seven

Textbook Definitions

The textbook definition of ethics refers to a desirable and appropriate value system of morals according to an individual or the society at large. Ethics deals with the purity of individuals and their intentions. Ethics serve as guidelines for analyzing what is considered to be appropriate or inappropriate behavior according to the situation. Showing the relationship between ethics with leadership, ethics becomes mostly about the leader's identity and the leader's role.

Ethical theories on political leadership discuss two main ideas: the first examining the actions and behavior of political leaders; and the second examining the personality and character of leaders. Although ethics is not essential to leadership, it does, however, provide a drive and influence with the political leader's ability to achieve a common goal, either it is to keep campaign promises, to maintain moral behavior or any other behavior. There is an ethical position of a political leader to treat constituents with respect as each political leader has a unique personality. The ethical environment is built and developed by a government agency, an ethics commission, which has an influential role in the organization and since political leaders influence in developing values. However, an effective and ethical leader has the following characteristics:

Dignity and respectfulness - There is respect for constituents. An ethical-political leader should not use the people as a medium to achieve their personal goals. Political leaders should respect constituent's feelings, decisions, and values. By respecting the people implies that the political leader is listening effectively to them, being compassionate to them, as well as being liberal in hearing opposing viewpoints.

Serving others - The ethical-political leader serves others. An ethical leader places their constituent's interests ahead of their interests. They are humanistic and act in a manner that is always fruitful to constituents.

Justice - The ethical-political leader is fair and just. An ethical leader must treat all constituents equally. There should be no personal bias. Wherever some constituents are treated differently, the ground for differential treatment should be fair, clear, and built on morality.

Honesty - The ethical-political leader is loyal and honest. Honesty is essential to be an ethical and effective leader. Honest leaders can be always relied upon and depended upon. They always earn the respect of constituents, an honest leader presents the fact and circumstances truly, and completely, no matter how critical and harmful, they do not misrepresent facts.

Political leadership must be all about values, and it is impossible to be an ethical leader if there is a lack of awareness and a concern for their values. Ethical political leadership has a moral and ethical aspect, which defines leadership; along with influencing their behavior.

Ethical leadership becomes greater than just having good character. The reality is that ethical leadership is complex. It is globalization, democratization, and incredible technological advances that are the cornerstone to ethical leadership. Politicians don't just see their constituents as followers, but rather as stakeholders that are striving towards the same purpose. It examines the context of that situation that the leader and constituents face, the leader's processes and skills, and the outcomes that result. Leaders are first and foremost members of their organizations and stakeholder groups. As such, their purpose, vision, and values are for the benefit of the entire organization and its key stakeholders.

Leaders see their constituents as not just followers, but rather as stakeholders striving to achieve that same common purpose, vision, and values. These follower and stakeholder constituents have their individuality and autonomy which must be respected to maintain a moral community. Ethical leaders embody the purpose, vision, and values of the organization and their constituents, within an understanding of ethical ideals. They connect the goals of the organization with that of the internal employees and external stakeholders. Leaders work to create conversation, where there is an understanding of different views, values, and the constituents' opinions. They are open to others' opinions and ideas because they know those ideas make the organization they are leading better.

The characteristics of ethical-political leaders in today's government system, ethics, and values are present at several levels for politicians to devote their time and energy to leading the process of value creation. This broader concept of ethical leadership empowers political leaders to incorporate and be responsible for their values and ethics. Understanding ethical leadership that is more complex and more useful than just a matter of "good character and values," it is important for political leaders to tell a compelling and moral story; along with being willing to live that story. This is a difficult task in government today where everyone lives in the public eye. So many political leaders fail to be willing to live by the high-minded stories they tell at election time where the focus has become based on the revelation of numerous scandals and inappropriate behaviors.

In many business organizations, employees are hired to fill a particular skill need with little regard to issues of integrity, something that continues to be missing among government agencies. Knowing the limits of the values and ethical principles that they live on allows for values to have limits. It is these limits on values where ethical leaders have an acute sense of their limits of the values and they are better prepared with solid reasons to defend their chosen course of action. Problems can arise when political leadership does not practice the limits of certain values.

Ethical leadership is about raising standards and creating value for their constituents. Although errors can occur, political leaders are ordinary people who are living their lives as examples of making the world a better place. Ethical leaders speak to us about our identity, what we are and what we can become, how we live and how we could live better.

If ethical leadership is to emerge in government then the value of the constituent and their responsibility principle becomes necessary. Outside of having the responsibility to constituents to become an ethical leader, commit to asking themselves the following questions:

- What are my most important values and principles?
- Does my calendar—how I spend my time and attention—reflect these values?
- What would my subordinates and peers say my values are?
- What mechanisms and processes have I designed to be sure that the people who work for me can push back against my authority?
- What could this organization do or ask me to do that would cause me to resign for ethical reasons?
- What do I want to accomplish with my leadership?
- What do I want people to say about my leadership when I am gone?
- Can I go home at the end of the day and tell my family about my leadership, and use my day's work to teach them to be ethical leaders?

The ability to ask these questions increases the opportunity for an increase in political ethical leadership. By adding the idea of ethical leadership government can become better by engaging leaders and the people in a conversation about what they see as ethical leadership. It is the values, purposes, principles, and an enterprising approach to a more disciplined way to think about how to make government and political leadership run more effectively, and to help to increase integrity.

Chapter Eight

Ethical Codes

In every organization from businesses to government, ethical codes of conduct exist as a guide for desirable behavior. Ethical codes are adopted by organizations to assist members in understanding the difference between 'right' and 'wrong' and in applying that understanding to their decisions. An ethical code generally implies documents at three levels: codes of business, codes of conduct for employees, and codes of professional practice.

Many companies use the phrases 'ethical code' and 'code of conduct' interchangeably, but in essence, many may be useful for making distinctions. A code of ethics often will start by setting out the values of the code and it will describe an organization's responsibility to its stakeholders or employees. The code is publicly available and addressed to anyone with an interest in the organization's activities and the way it does business. It will include details of how the company plans to implement its values and vision, as well as guidance to staff on ethical standards and how to achieve them. However, a code of conduct is generally addressed to and intended for employees alone. It usually sets out restrictions on behavior and will be far more compliance or rules focused than value or principle-focused. This code is also good for those that are a part of a Non-Governmental Organization.

A code of practice is adopted by a profession or by a governmental or non-governmental organization to regulate that profession. A code of practice may be styled as a code of their professional responsibility, which discusses difficult issues or scenarios, difficult decisions that will often need to be made, and provide a clear account of what behavior is considered "ethical" or "correct" or "right" in the circumstances. In a membership context, failure to comply with a code of practice can result in expulsion from the professional organization. It is a principle that is provided for those within the organization. The working definition of a principle is the values, standards, or rules of behavior that guide the decisions, procedures, and systems of an organization in a way that will contribute to the welfare of its key stakeholders, and respects the rights of all constituents affected by its operations.

In response to government agencies maintaining a code of ethics, Washington established in 2009, the Transparency and Open Government to strengthen democracy by providing the following definitions:

- *Government should be transparent.* Transparency promotes accountability and provides information for citizens about what their Government is doing. Information maintained by the Federal Government is a national asset. My Administration will take appropriate action, consistent with law and policy, to disclose information rapidly in forms that the public can readily find and use. Executive departments and agencies should harness new technologies to put information about their operations and decisions online and readily available to the public. Executive departments and agencies should also solicit public feedback to identify information of greatest use to the public.

- *Government should be participatory.* Public engagement enhances the Government's effectiveness and improves the quality of its decisions. Knowledge is widely dispersed in society, and public officials benefit from having access to that dispersed knowledge. Executive departments and agencies should offer Americans increased opportunities to participate in policymaking and to provide their Government with the benefits of their collective expertise and information. Executive departments and agencies should also solicit public input on how we can increase and improve opportunities for public participation in Government.
- *Government should be collaborative.* Collaboration actively engages Americans in the work of their Government. Executive departments and agencies should use innovative tools, methods, and systems to cooperate among themselves, across all levels of Government, and with nonprofit organizations, businesses, and individuals in the private sector. Executive departments and agencies should solicit public feedback to assess and improve their level of collaboration and to identify new opportunities for cooperation.

In an effort toward a commitment to build ethics in government, other measures were put in place through the Hatch Act. The Hatch Act, 5 U.S.C. §§ 7321-7326 puts limits on certain political activities of most executive branch employees while on duty or in the Federal workplace. It also prohibits soliciting or receiving political contributions.

Through the establishment of ethical codes of conduct are

standards, especially with political leadership. According to the United States House of Representatives, the Code of Ethics for Government Service is explicit when examining responsibility and behavior, these standards are as follows:

Any person in Government service should:

- Put loyalty to the highest moral principles and country above loyalty to Government persons, parties, or departments.

- Uphold the Constitution, laws, and legal regulations of the United States and all governments therein and never become a party to their evasion.

- Give a full day's labor for a full day's pay; giving to the performance of his duties his earnest effort and best thought.

- Seek to find and employ more efficient and economical ways of getting tasks accomplished.

- Never discriminate unfairly by the dispensing of special favors or privileges to anyone, whether for remuneration or not; and never accept for himself or his family, favors or benefits under circumstances which might be construed by reasonable persons as influencing the performance of his governmental duties.

- Make no private promises of any kind binding upon the duties of office, since a Government employee has no private word which can be binding on public duty.

- Engage in no business with the Government, either directly or indirectly which is inconsistent with the conscientious performance of his governmental duties.

- Never use any information coming to him confidentially in the performance of governmental duties as a means for making a private profit.

- Expose corruption wherever discovered.
- Uphold these principles, ever conscious that public office is a public trust.

Voters' dissatisfaction with political parties, politics, and politicians is how democracy works. By increasing further when major corruption scandals are discovered ultimately negatively impacts the effectiveness of democracy. The discovery of corruption practices, of corrupt officials and corrupt politicians, has a profound impact on the political system, not only because it significantly affects the electoral process for political parties, but more importantly it changes the peoples' perception of the political system.

By establishing an ethical standard for political parties and politicians puts accountability and response as a significant fact that democracy is not working well. Corruption, in particular, creates another concern for democracy. This is due to corrupt politicians can utilize for their electoral campaigns their illicitly obtained resources that were acquired as an advantage over the other candidates, while improving their chances to be elected. By doing so, corrupt candidates distort electoral competition, prevent the people's will from being properly expressed, and by doing so, they violate the spirit of democracy. And to the extent that it violates the spirit of democracy, corruption poses a direct threatens democracy. However, corruption is not the only threat to democracy. Any form of legislative misconduct undermines the public trust in the democratic system and by doing so, it poses an indirect threat to the democratic system's legitimacy. The creation of ethical codes is one way as a representative attempt to regulate the behavior of politicians and to rebuild public trust in the political system.

Chapter Nine

Trust Factor

There has been a consistent pattern where trust has become broken among politics. According to a Pew Research Poll, public trust in government remains at historic lows. In a survey conducted in February 2014, 24% stated that they trust the government in Washington always or most of the time.

In 1976, when just a third said the government did right most or all the time, however from the 1980s through the 1990s, there have been spikes in the amount of patriotism, with the greatest being just after September 11, 2001. By the year 2011, patriotism continued to drop due to a budget that couldn't be balanced by Congress and America's credit downgrade.

Today, the government is being measured by the frustrations that have plagued with ineffectiveness and partisanship over Washington and political leaders' inability to not work on their battles but rather to work for the average people. For many, the lack of trust has become born not because of apprehension of what government may do, but instead because Congress isn't doing anything at all.

The views of Washington may be due to politicians no longer thinking about the people any longer. The thinking becomes what's good for the nation isn't good for Congress. This type of thinking influences lobbyists and special interests. It isn't about a political party, but instead, it's the instructional and structural organization that is causing the people to distrust the government. Much of this may be due to constant infighting that the lack of trust is becoming deeper and more prevailing.

Jimmy Carter had once said: "Government cannot solve our problems, it cannot set our goals, and it cannot define our vision. Government cannot eliminate poverty or provide a bountiful economy or reduce inflation or save our cities or cure illiteracy or provide energy. And government cannot mandate goodness." However, since Watergate, Democrats like Jimmy Carter and Bill Clinton have expressed very little confidence in government, while Republicans like Ronald Reagan expressed outright contempt. The decline of trust is what matters in government. The reason for such concerns is that such thinking has a profound effect on American politics, while it defines the political landscape over the last several decades within the nation.

Political candidates have capitalized on the distrust in Washington. In September 2000, George W. Bush had difficulty with his campaign. Al Gore emerged from the Democratic Convention with fire. Gore's vice president, Joseph Lieberman who was a pro-business and the first Jewish candidate for national office, won high praise from the people. The Democratic Party successfully reengaged elements of their party's coalition, mostly women, union members, and racial minorities.

Even with such successes, the American people have since this election has lost their faith in the government to implement and administer public policy. Such change in public opinion has changed greatly over the last forty years. People began to think about government in terms of redistributive programs instead of universal programs, this has caused less trust in the federal government. It takes political trust in general, a concept that many think they understand until asked to define it. Some consider it to be a commodity that helps political leaders to achieve their goals, while others define it as a people's willingness to follow the political leadership of others.

Political trust is instead a shared moral community of both

political and social agreement of values that the people should pursue. People who live in more trusting societies tend to trust the government more than those living in less trusting societies. We can easily define trust as people trusting people. However, those who do not trust the government. The political and social aspects of trust do differ. Social trust affects how an individual votes or participates more actively in politics, while a political trust doesn't. Political trust may be defined by the degree to which people perceive that the government is producing outcomes that are consistent with their expectations. Trust in government is a broad term and what the people concern themselves with in political trust is that policy ends are more important than policy means. Political trust is a reflection of how positively the people perceive government performance that is relative to their expectations.

Within democracies, political trust is essential to representing all people. Political trust doesn't mean that there is trust in an individual political leader. Instead, people can trust the government and not the political leader. During Bill Clinton's six-year term as president, the people had a decreased view of his trustworthiness, while the people may have trusted Jimmy Carter personally because he made his ethics an important part of his political leadership, however, most did not trust the government. This was due to during Carter's term in office performance was viewed as poor by the people. More often, those who are trustful of the political leader tend to be trustful of the government. However, there isn't always a guaranteed relationship between trust being present in government will also be present in a political leader. Although what may have an increased relationship is that regaining trust, should it occur, will not come from a single election, political leader, or policy. Rather it may be built by the people over repeated actions and time.

Chapter Ten

Reforming Government

We often hear about political issues, events, and news on politicians both at the local, state, and national levels. One of the principal reasons for it being everywhere is due to the focus that is placed on it by media attention. What the people hear on the news, the stories that are covered, and how these stories are reported becoming crucial to understanding how the people are governed. Many working in politics recognize that people receive their information through the media, this includes social media. However, it was the early newspapers that had focused on political ideologies or yellow journalism, where bold headlines were used to entertain and to appeal to a wider audience.

Politics is often a game of wits. However, the media has found ways to taint a politician's reputation as being unethical. With unreliable truths, he continued to hold to maintaining an ethical principle, as the people learn about the case after case of corruption that may be built on idiosyncratic standards of public corruption. This is where the need for political reformers becomes a needed entity in politics. A political reformer holds the following criteria:

- Political reform means improving the laws and constitutions following the expectations of the public. Requirements of all the segments of the society are included in 'public expectations.' In a democracy, everybody bears equal rights of a single vote, but their equal participation in the decision-making process of the state is not ensured. Hence, for political reform to ensure minimum economic equity is needed;

- Political reform means evolving such an electoral system by which gentility could be empowered in the state machinery; and
- Political reform means evolving such a constitution of a political party, so that the party working through that constitution may be able to work for political reforms.

Even still, the media still looks for unbounded ways to hold politicians accountable for unethical behavior. This is something that I like to call the ham sandwich conviction, where any one of us, even a person who lives a simple life, could be found guilty of breaking some kind of law in our lifetime. However, when there isn't much negative behavior to find on a person, especially one serving in public office, it's the media's way of trying to build a case of wrongdoing. Instead, the media did whatever possible to plaque a politician's image to bring people to believe that that they could be just as corrupt as so many other politicians before them. Speculation that brings about untrue stories to believe, is the downfall of working in public office.

Finding political reformers is slowly taking shape in government, but the price is higher. It is common to hear of the importance of politicians giving endorsements for others running for office. It becomes so personal, that they are courted by other politicians as a means for officials to give fair warning of the repercussions that could happen to them for not endorsing. There is a give-and-take methodology to holding public office. The message is simple: outlining a good relationship with another politician, especially one of higher office, becomes seen as beneficial for the endorser's future ambition. This isn't always true. Maintaining a "no strings attached" philosophy, a plan was executed to ignore such means is the desired plan, where there are more answers than there are questions, including best understanding the role of political parties.

To best understand how political parties affect reform thinking. Looking into how parties were developed helps to understand the ideology for its movement. We see it begin in 1787, where a group of people began calling themselves the Federalists. This was the first United States political party. In 1796, anti-Federalists gathered around Jefferson. Members of Jefferson's group called themselves Democratic-Republicans. Political parties were not held favorable to many holding public offices. The idea of being a part of a political party strongly comes out of a few ideas. Some of these ideas include ideology, policy position, and public acceptance, as history repeats itself.

Political parties have changed the landscape of how candidates run for election. Often built on the idea that to be successful and to hold office, one must be supported by either the Democratic or Republican party. Over the years since its establishment, political parties such as the Republican Party sharply are taking a path toward being diminished. The current state of the Republican Party is changing, with candidates slowly becoming split between conservatives and liberals. A similar situation had occurred during the time of Abraham Lincoln, as the Whig Party would become a party made up of conservatives and liberals. The change of political views brought about the creation of the Republican Party.

The Orthodox Conservative ways that were a driving force in American public policy, have begun to make the Republican Party less popular among the people. Not since Dwight Eisenhower, has the Republican Party has found a decrease in a candidate supporting the foundations such as free trade and supporting the value to military alliances. The idea of every man is created equal, as the source of being every man's freedom and dignity. This was the idea of building the Republican Party more than a hundred years ago, and the reason for why the nation was founded. When the foundations on God are decreased and an increased focus on transgender issues begins to exist, this is when the signs of destruction may be seen of the Republican Party. With fewer and fewer candidates supporting the foundations of conservatism the idea of government created by the people, for the people has less purpose. Instead, the conservative candidate diminishes, along with the formation of its party. This change in a candidate may be seen during the time of the presidency of Dwight Eisenhower.

In a 1909 address that President Eisenhower gave, which stated that "the reader should bear in mind that the Republican Party was breaking up into conservative and liberal factions." As Roosevelt changed his position from Republican to Democratic, the decision was an important step, one that would determine his political standing for life. Choosing one party over another, the idea is to remain a life member of that party. It is a decision that may often lead to the diminishing of the Republican Party, one where over time, history may repeat itself, as the party struggles to maintain strength during elections. It was similar diminishes that were found during the development of the Whig Party and its diminishing toward becoming the Republican Party and its principle goal for stopping the expansion of slavery.

The Republican Party had a principal goal, that goal was to stop the expansion of slavery into the western territories. Abraham Lincoln, the sixteenth president of the United States, had been involved with the Whig Party, which was disintegrating due, in large part, to sectional rivalries. Since Lincoln was personally opposed to slavery, he found the Republican Party platform much to his liking. George Washington, the first president of the United States, had no desire to be a part of a political party and hoped that they would never be formed. Washington was strongly admired for his strong leadership qualities. Washington was unanimously elected president in the first two national elections. He oversaw the creation of a strong, well-financed national government that maintained neutrality in wars such as the French Revolutionary War. Washington suppressed the Whiskey Rebellion and won acceptance among

Americans of all types. Washington's incumbency established many precedents, still in use today. This was completed without the support of Washington's participation in a political party and developing its brand today.

Political parties carry an idea, a notion, and a brand that is presented to the voter that markets candidates and current elected officials, this is important when providing establishment support to political candidates in their quest for being elected. Brands are important since they provide information on the character and identity of products and companies. In this case, the product is the candidate. The loss of Republican candidates has been attributed to a fundamentally flawed candidate who has emerged into the primaries with a tarnished brand. The Republican Party has become popularized with negativity before a campaign has begun. The popularized negativity found among the Republican Party is strong enough, that it can no longer be able to sustain its most important product, a candidate.

Branding, especially among political parties, becomes essential to the ability to bringing the people to want to become a part of their vision and mission. The subconscious mind is as powerful as a vote. For a candidate as part of a tarnished brand, the ability to impact decision-making through the ability to reach the people through emotional and rational sides of an individual. It is essential to connect stories that maximize the subconscious mind to win an election. However, the Republican Party may consider using storytelling as a major pathway into rebranding the party.

Storytelling may be used in three paths, habits, beliefs, and stories, in the following ways:

- *Habits* are our routines in life. Neuroscience supports that habits become the autopilot for our decisions, which is why habits are so difficult to break. It also demonstrates why the habit of telling the same story becomes a major part of how we act and view our life;
- *Beliefs* are the conclusions we make by living life. It

is important to understand that all beliefs are not equal. If we attach emotion to a belief, then that belief becomes more important to us. Often these beliefs are referred to as our core principles and values; and

- Stories impact beliefs because one of the components of a story is *emotion.* It is often the emotional impact of a story that has the most profound impact on the success of the story. Neuroscience supports why emotions play such a critical role in storytelling.

Brands are symbols that provide signals about the identity of a product. The ability of the Republican Party to reinvent its brand will be challenging. In a survey conducted of 1200 U.S. voters, using fourteen positive brand words and phrases, to tell researchers which phrases were better to describe the party, Republican and Democrat. The Democrat Party ranked increasingly higher than the Republican Party in thirteen of the fourteen phrases. Several key areas, including: "offering hope of a vision for the future," "cares about people like me," "clearly explains how its actions will benefit me," "understands issues facing the middle class," "works to bring about change," "honest and ethical" and "smart and innovative" Other key words, such as hopeful, caring, beneficial, understanding, changing, ethical, and innovative had a high correlation or relationship as brand signals of the Democratic Party. The brand signals found to have a strong relationship to the Democratic Party would align with important factors that attribute to a favorable view of Nike and its ability to have the most appealing colors, in turn to being the least important factor for buying athletic shoes.

The Republican Party may have a significant brand issue. It is essential to correct it through immediate action, which may mean the party's brand and the image is necessary for recovery. For any brand that has lost a positive image, establishing what the party stands for may mean relating to the concerns that matter deeply to the consumer while differentiating itself from the Democratic Party. Communicating the differences in a way that is simple and easy to understand, but more importantly, introducing a leader who reflects on core values, as well as addressing the emotional and rational side, habits, beliefs, and emotions, may be needed to re-build the Republican Party brand and its diminish.

More and more, we see that politics and its elections are being driven by party lines. This is what I like to call red versus blue. Many involved as political reformers will take a side, however, will easily switch from the red to the blue and vice versa. The loyalty isn't to a political party. That's not the solemn vow, but instead, the oath is believed to be of the people. To understand where the red and blue came from, the history of these colors is of great interest to understanding why political reformers will keep loyalty to a political party and its color at bay.

Chapter Eleven

Election Maps

In early October of 1976, the month before the map was to debut live on election night. At the urging of anchor John Chancellor, NBC had constructed a map to illustrate, in vivid blue and red, which states supported Republican incumbent Gerald Ford, and which voters supported Democratic challenger Jimmy Carter. Although the test run didn't go well. The electoral map was supported by a sturdy wood frame and the front of each state was plastic. With thousands of bulbs, the map started to melt when we turned all the lights on. It was then that NBC brought in a large interior air conditioning and fans to put behind the map to cool it. This was the beginning of how red and blue came about during elections.

Since its beginnings, blue was red and red was blue and they changed back and forth from election to election and network to network. The notion that there were "red states" and "blue states," however, red and blue didn't become permanent until the year 2000. In the election of Bush v. Gore, not only did it give the people an idea as to who was winning, but it also gave an understanding to the Electoral College. It also led to a controversial Supreme Court ruling and a heightened level of polarization that has intensified ever since.

Twelve years later, in the final days of a presidential race deemed too close to call, we know this much about election night Nov. 6: The West Coast, the Northeast, and much of the upper Midwest will be bathed in blue. With some notable exceptions, the geographic center of the nation would be awash of red, as well as the South. Ultimately, it is a handful of states, which will start the evening in shades of neutral and shift, one by one, to red or blue. This is what will determine who wins. When states have not been determined as red or blue, they are instead purple.

When looking at the maps on television and websites during election night, along with in newspapers the next morning, they will look alike. We won't have to switch our thinking as we switch channels, wondering which candidate is blue and which is red. Before the election of 2000, there was no uniformity in the maps that television stations, newspapers, or magazines used to illustrate presidential elections. Pretty much everyone embraced red and blue, but rather which color represented which party varied, sometimes by the organization, and other times by election cycle. However, the role of social media sites such as Facebook has become a greater influence on how people feel about elections.

Facebook's role in providing Americans with political news has never been stronger, or more controversial. Social media can create a way where users see posts only from like-minded friends and media sources. Facebook encourages users to "keep an open mind" by seeking out posts that don't appear in their feeds.

To demonstrate how reality may differ for different Facebook users, The Wall Street Journal created two feeds, one "blue," and the other "red." If a source appears in the red feed, a majority of the articles shared from the source were classified as "very conservatively aligned" in a large 2015 Facebook study. For the blue feed, a majority of each source's articles aligned "very liberal." These aren't intended to resemble actual individual news feeds. Instead, they are rare side-by-side looks at real conversations from different perspectives. However, most interesting is the use of red and blue.

During a Monday night presidential debate, both Hilary

Clinton and Donald Trump had used their signature styles. However, what made this debate quite different from many is that Clinton wore a bright pantsuit; Trump donned a colorful tie, crisp white shirt, and, of course, a spray tan, but one detail stood out: The candidates wore colors generally associated with the other's political party. Clinton selected a warm, crimson ensemble in traditional Republican red, whereas Trump chose a tie in royal blue, a rallying color for the Democratic Party. This surprising switch was immediately noted on social media:

According to the field of color psychology, there are several interesting insights as to using the opposite color of a candidate's political party. For example, red can help you win. Red is generally associated with warmth, courage, willpower, speed, and assertiveness, red has been found to tip the winner scales at sporting events because it's touted to increase players' aggression and dominance. Red also increases attraction. Red, relative to other achromatic and chromatic colors, leads men to view women as more attractive and more sexually desirable." The hypothesis: Humans may be conditioned to associate color with fertility. The same researchers found a few years later that human reactions become both faster and more forceful to the color because and may be seen as a dangerous signal. Humans flush when they are angry or preparing for the attack. People are acutely aware of such reddening in others and its implications. This is quite different from blue, which helps with creative thinking.

In 2009, Scientists from the University of British Columbia found that blue is the best color for increasing creative thinking. By associating blue with the sky, the ocean, and water, most people associate blue with openness, peace, and tranquility. Blue can make people feel safe about being creative and exploratory. It is also the most popular color.

In 2012, a study completed at the University of Maryland surveyed nearly 2,000 men and women what their favorite color was and found that blue scored highest across sexes, with 42 percent of men preferring blue and 29 percent of women touting it as their preferred shade across age, race, and education level. Although color might not have played a major part in the debate, during an election in which appearance and looks are integral, every outfit counts. Although red and blue have become popularized on social media, there is a history behind the use of color in politics.

Political colors are used to represent a political party, either officially or unofficially. Parties in different countries with similar ideologies sometimes use similar colors. For example, the color red symbolizes left-wing ideologies in many countries. However, the political associations of a given color vary from country to country. For example, red is also the color is associated with the conservative Republican Party in the United States. Politicians making public appearances will often identify themselves by wearing rosettes, flowers, or ties in the color of their political party. The following list of colors has represented political parties over the years.

- *Black-* Black is primarily associated with anarchism;
- *Blue-* Blue is usually associated with conservatives parties, originating from its use by the Tory party, the predecessor of the Conservative Party, in the United Kingdom;
- *Brown-* Brown is sometimes used to describe the opposite of green parties, that is, to describe parties that care little about pollution;
- *Buff-* Buff was the color of the Whig faction in British politics from the early 18th century until the middle of the 19th century. As such it is sometimes used to represent the current political left. This was in opposition to blue, which represented the Tories and then the Conservatives and political right;
- *Grey-* Grey is often used to represent Independent politicians;
- *Green-* Green is the color for green politics, Green parties, and environmentalist movements worldwide;

-    *Orange-* Orange is the traditional color of the Christian Democrats, and it can also represent various kinds of populist parties;

-    *Pink-* Pink is sometimes used by social-democratic parties, such as in France and Portugal. The more traditional color of social democracy is red. This is because social democracy is descended from the democratic socialist movement), but some countries have large social-democratic parties alongside large socialist or communist parties so that it would be confusing for them all to use red. Social democrats are usually the ones who give up red in favor of a different color. Pink is often chosen because it is seen as a softer, less aggressive version of red, in the same way, that social democracy is more centrist and less militant than socialism;

-    *Purple-* Although purple has some older associations with monarchism, it is the most prominent color that is not traditionally connected to any major contemporary ideology. As such, it is sometimes used to represent a mix of different ideologies or new protest movements that are critical of all previously-existing parties;

-    *Red-* Red is traditionally associated with socialism and communism. The oldest symbol of socialism, and by extension, communism, is the Red Flag. The color red was generally associated with the monarchy or the Church due to the symbolism and association of Christ's blood. The color red was chosen to represent the blood of the workers who died in the struggle against capitalism. All major socialist and communist alliances and organizations included the First, Second, and Third Internationals, which used red as their official color. The association between the color red and communism is particularly strong. Communists use red much more often and more extensively than other ideologies use their respective traditional colors;

-    *White-* White in politics has been associated with

independent politicians; and
- *Yellow-* Yellow is the color most commonly associated with liberalism. It is the official color of the Alliance of Liberals and Democrats for Europe (ALDE), as well as being the color of liberal parties in Germany, Romania, Estonia, and the United Kingdom, the Liberal Democrats. Yellow or gold, usually together with blue or purple, is also often used to represent libertarianism.

As we become more technological, the use of red and blue on social media has been revolutionizing political communication, campaigning, and influencing voter choice. As the United States becomes more involved in the digital age, the impact of red, blue, and other colors used to represent political parties, will become more profound to our decision-making. In many ways, it is much like the influence that Coke-a-Cola commercials had on the consumer. The more that we became exposed to the product, the more likely we would buy into what they were selling. Social media and the use of color psychology with political candidates are doing something quite similar to the voter, otherwise known as the age of social media transparency.

Chapter Twelve

Social Media Age

The use of media such as newspapers, opinion columns, and blogs; for many politicians may often bring fear. This fear is brought on because of a loss of power to control what is being said about the many men and women who hold public office. However, just as easily as a media source could be hurtful to a politician, it can also help them. This is especially true during elections where attaining endorsements may be seen as crucial. Even with this thinking, there has yet to be evidence to show that the use of newspapers has made a difference in how people vote. With as much publicity being used between social and print, sources such as newspapers can't control their readers. Although with the decline in newspapers fast approaching and social media replacing much of how people receive information, there have been many politicians who are taking to their cell phones and computers.

After taking office, many in politics, including reformers, are using social media to communicate directly to the people. The use of social media can also increase transparency. Transparency has been a key goal for candidates when running for public office and for many people, the ability to use social media has been a 'breath of fresh air.' It's unheard of for a politician to be attainable to the people. However, not only does the use of social media increase communication and transparency, but it also increases credibility. Using social media presence as a public forum to the people has led politicians to have more direct contact with the city and its people. Instantly, politicians can get his message out without filters and can relay exactly what he wants to say without it being altered. Facebook and Twitter are natural among politicians at all levels of government.

A report issued by the Congressional Research Service concluded that members of Congress are rapidly and avidly taking to forms of social media that did not exist fifteen years ago. The advantages for each are the distribution immediate speed at a minimal cost. Back in 2010, surveys had shown 205 of five hundred thirty-eight members of Congress on Twitter accounts and three hundred and forty-nine on Facebook with the numbers growing. Among members of Congress, one study noted usage varied greatly. During a two-month study, sixteen congressmen tweeted at least one hundred times in sixty days, including one who alone was approximately two hundred and ninety tweets.

Facebook was great in organizing supporters, for events; while he used Twitter to specialize in getting messages to supporters very quickly. Traditional means were still important to him. Using interviews with the press and public appearances allowed for the people to be there without actually physically being in the room. It was a unique way of connecting. For politicians, both reformers and non-reformers, are making appearances across the nation can keep up with the momentum of delivering information to the people through social media. It also allowed for it to be a voice for the people.

With a business approach, politicians can use the strength of their followers to build new ones. The use of social media affords to spread the message out much further. Politicians can make announcements and connect the people to articles in the newspaper that directly affected them and the city's future while improving public service. Using social media to reconnect with the city and to learn more about what they wanted, politicians, especially reformers, can listen to their constituency's problems more directly. They can show their supporters exactly what they and what the government is doing to help. One example has been over the winter months. Using the quote: "There isn't such thing as bad weather, only different types of good weather" - an optimist. Nevertheless, we are plowing!" Political reformers can drive the message to all that treating the streets was being accomplished.

Political reformers are using social media in much the same way businesses do: by 'trying to convince the public to embrace something.' In this sense, reformers can provide a public perception by broadcasting both positive and some not-so-positive information via social media outlets.

One way to communicating and transparency, while increasing credibility has been through writing. Writing on topics such as endorsements, the economy, health care coverage, veterans, gun reform, and current issues that have directly affected the people. Political reformers are building a different type of platform outside of the political arena. Instead, their focus has been on bringing awareness by using a perspective that many do not have a chance to learn about through their own local and state politicians. In other ways, political reformers are continuing to brand the city through writing monthly opinion blogs. Much of what is expressed, while bringing forth insight into what has impacted lives.

With each method of communication, this politician used not only social media to instill confidence within his community, but he also used his writing on blogs to increase his presence to the people. Even as he began his career as mayor he not only chose to provide professionalism but also expressing his thoughts as to the challenges that were ahead of his head.

In another post, Endorsements Hardly Matter, a political reformer discussed how endorsements should be used when they will improve the lives of their constituents; along with how the idea of endorsements being the 'Holy Grail of campaign momentum' have ultimately become a thing of the past. This way of communicating to the people a view that can be respected. It shows that the decisions being able to are being considered first before acting upon them. Something at times politicians' neglect to achieve.

As a political reformer, being active in using social media became a winning strategy for many holding public offices, this is especially true during an election year. Although veteran politicians are beginning to become accustomed to the use of Twitter and Facebook, what political reformers can accomplish outweighs the years before working campaigns. Indeed, social media can be a powerful tool for modern politicians. Connecting with voters on an individual basis is so important, and with social networking sites, a politician doesn't have to organize a door-to-door neighborhood campaign to achieve that connection.

PART IV

Chapter Thirteen

Truth Behind Lying In Politics

We watch with fascination as candidates for the world's most powerful candidates potentially speak falsehoods and allegations of dishonesty. It's a challenge to know if a politician is lying. Many of us have given little thought to our lies and to how they compare with politicians' deceits.

For more than two decades, researchers of different stripes have examined humanity's less-than-truthful underbelly. This is what they have found: We all stretch the truth. We learned to deceive as toddlers. We rationalize the fabrications that benefit us. We tell little white lies daily that make others feel good.

Now magnify that to how politicians may distort the truth more often, use more self-justifications, and deceive in larger ways, and with more consequences, experts in psychology and political science.

There is more worry about lying in public life. This is especially true for politicians than ever before. When lies succeed, they make it more tempting to lie. Lies can stick. They can have a lingering effect, even if they are debunked, and deception starts early.

Children learn to lie at an average of about 3 years old, often when they realize that other people don't know what they are thinking.

There is extensive research on children and lying. Lee set up an experiment in a video-monitored room and would tell children there was they can have that's behind them, but they can only get it if they don't peek. Then the adult is called out of the room, returns a minute later and asks if they peeked.

At age 2, only 30 percent lie. At age 3, half do. By 5 or 6, 90 percent of the kids lie and Lee said he worries about the 10 percent who don't lie. We explicitly teach our kids to tell white lies, with parental coaching about things like saying how much they love gifts from grandma, and it's a lesson most of them only get around age 6 or older.

In 1996, DePaulo, author of "The How's and Whys of Lies," put recorders on students for a week and found they lied, on average, in every third conversation of 10 minutes or more. For adults, it was once every five conversations. A few years later, Robert Feldman at the University of Massachusetts taped students in conversations with total strangers and got similar results with the participants not realizing they were lying until they watched themselves. We lie constantly. The problem is there are many shades of truth-bending. Experts split on whether to count white lies and "social lubrication" that makes civilized operate. When your spouse tells you that you don't look fat in that outfit when you do, does it really do any harm?

There's a difference between white lies and real lies. Some lies fall under politeness norms and are not very harmful. Other lies are self-interested and those are the harmful ones. Those are the ones that harm relationships, harm trust. However, others see no distinction: It doesn't matter if the attempt was motivated by good intentions and it doesn't matter if the lie is about something little. Regardless, society rewards people for white lies.

We're trained to be deceptive Feldman said. "If we're not, if we're totally truthful all the time that's not a good thing, there's a price to be paid for that. We don't like people who tell us the truth all the time. From there it's only a small leap to what politicians do.

The lies that we accept from politicians right now are lies that are seen as acceptable because it's what we want to hear, such as a spouse saying that an outfit flatters you. Or perhaps we feel that lying is necessary. People want their politicians to lie to them. The reason that people want their politicians to lie them is that people care about politics. Washington is a dirty place and that lying is very helpful to get your policies implemented.

When people deceive beyond white lies, they spend a lot of effort justifying and rationalizing what they are doing. They engage in something we call justified dishonesty. It happens when people's desire to be ethical clashes with the desire to profit or get something. In that case people are willing to lie just a bit just long as it seems legitimate ad with a rationale to lie. There is the thinking that it's okay and rationalizing that there is a meaningful purpose. Politicians convince themselves that the ends justify the means and the reasons they are doing it.

Dishonesty is contagious. Although most people want to be honest. The public tends to believe things – even if they are false – that confirms what we already believe" and come from news sources and partisans that they already trust and agree with, however, politicians should be held up to a higher standard. Over the decades, they and the government have been more deceitful and unwilling to tell the public something that could hurt them politically. When President Dwight Eisenhower misled the public about a spy plane captured by the Soviet Union, lying was the exception. By the time President Bill Clinton strained the meaning of the word "is" testifying before a grand jury, it was more common. In Washington, deception is the gift that keeps on giving. However, there's a high cost in everyday society – a loss of trust that is difficult to regain – when someone is discovered to be lying. There are also costs to the liar. The effect of deception on the body and brain and how much energy it takes to create and maintain a lie causes stress. The Marines share a belief and practice system that works.

Semper Fi is the Marine Corps motto which means "Always Faithful." This phrase encompasses the Marines' dedication to their country, their fellow Marines, and their families. Marines are expected to live up to this motto both in and uniform. Although it may not be a public office, Marines take an oath to keeping public trust that is similar to political oaths to protect and to serve.

Chapter Fourteen

What Is An Oath?

An oath is defined as an oath as a ritual act, or more specifically a "speech act." It is an oath that includes one kind of speech act. Taking an oath expresses a specific intention to others, using words like "I promise to" or "I swear that." The intention when taking an oath is not limited to the moment someone articulates the words of the oath. Oath-taking is also about the intention in the future to commit to acting a certain way. One example is the vows taken by couples during their wedding in front of witnesses. British philosopher John L. Austin called oaths "performance utterances."

The engaged couple, for example, declares to marry each other by speaking their vows to one another. They make a deliberate choice of their own free will. However, it was the Roman soldiers who first gave their allegiance. The ritual of taking oaths goes back centuries in Western Europe. In antiquity, oaths were often demanded of religious and governmental leaders, as well as those in certain professions. In ancient Rome, oaths were also demanded of soldiers.

The most solemn military oath – directly invoking the Roman gods – was the "sacramental." By this oath, soldiers swore allegiance to their specific general or commanding consul and, later, to the emperor. Disobedience could earn severe punishments.

A tapestry scene showing swearing oath on holy relics to William, Duke of Normandy. Myrabella via Wikimedia Commons

On some occasions, oath-breaking was tested by resorting to divine intervention. The virgin goddess Vesta was one of the most important in Roman religion. Her priestesses, the Vestals, or Vestal Virgins, therefore took an oath of chastity for their 30-year term of service tending to the ever-burning sacred fire of Rome, Vesta's sacred hearth, as well as other rites.

Vestals accused of breaking that oath were judged by the high priest of Rome. Since a priestess was a sacred person, her blood could not be shed. If found guilty, the priestess was buried alive, with a lamp and a little food, and left to the judgment of Vesta. If any condemned Vestal were innocent, it was believed that surely the goddess would free her from her living death, which began in the middle Ages

In medieval Europe, Christians continued to take oaths. The religious and secular worlds were closely interconnected for most of these centuries, and most oaths referred to Christian beliefs.

In the early middle Ages, Christians took oaths in the name of God, often while holding a religious object like a relic of a saint or a book of the Gospels. In most cases, oaths were not strictly person-to-person but involved the wider community in some important way. Kings took coronation oaths, swearing to rule justly and safeguard the people of the kingdom; lesser nobles took oaths of fealty to greater nobles, often for protection and material advantage.

Religious leaders like bishops and abbots also became part of this oath-based system, since there was a secular jurisdiction over important tracts of land. Breaking an oath was believed to bring down the wrath of God in time, but other than that, upholding one's personal honor and reputation within the local community was a key consideration.

Until the early 13th century, Christian rites would accompany the earlier Germanic practice of trial by ordeal. In these earlier centuries, most local people accused of a crime could be found not guilty by compurgation – that is, through oaths made by other respected members of the community testifying to the accused's honest character.

In other cases, often involving strangers to the local community, the accused could be cleared only by divine intervention. After a night of fasting and prayer, the accused would undergo a physical ordeal, like carrying a heated block of iron over a set number of steps or being thrown into a pond to sink or float.

If the accused did not develop blisters or was "accepted" by the water and sank, that was understood as God's declaration of his innocence. As time went on, scholars and ordinary people increasingly criticized the reliability of trials by ordeal. By the 13th century, the procedures of the court trial were defined and adopted, both in canon law, that is, the church law, and in secular law. Oaths matter when looking at the history of why they were developed for those serving in public office.

When drafting the U.S. Constitution in 1787, the Founding

Fathers rejected some of the legal practices of the British system of law. One such rejection was of the "religious test." In Great Britain, all office holders had to affirm the religious doctrines of the Church of England. But in the independent United States, there was to be no such religious restriction placed on federal officeholders. Preserving religious liberty was a primary concern protected by the Constitution.

One of the British legal practices the Founding Fathers did include in the Constitution was the swearing of oaths upon entering federal governmental service. However, these oaths were not taken to pledge loyalty to a single monarch, but to "protect and defend" the Constitution itself, but "swearing-in ceremonies" communicate far more. Supreme Court justices take two oaths, one judicial, and the other constitutional. The oath ceremony is still a serious performative utterance.

Appointees take these oaths in front of witnesses, who are themselves, representative of the entire community, the appointees will serve. Appointees to the Supreme Court commit themselves, not to a partisan political agenda, and not to a cult of personality or to the judgment of popular opinion. They commit themselves to "protect and defend the Constitution" and "administer justice without respect to persons ... faithfully and impartially."

Justices might be impeached by Congress for failing in "good behavior." However, in practice, justices serve for life, until death or retirement, and are bound in good conscience to carry out their "duties" as they have sworn to do. It is the conscience of appointees, not the preservation of their reputations, has been that the focus of these "oaths of office" for approximately 250 years.

Chapter Fifteen

Loyalty Oaths

A loyalty oath is a declaration by an individual of allegiance to a government and its institutions and a disavowal of support for foreign ideologies or associations.

The constitutionality of loyalty oaths is part of the larger struggle between the power of government to regulate perceived threats to national security and the First Amendment rights of citizens to speak and to associate freely. Over the history of early America, Loyalty Oaths were essential, since they helped the United States when it became a self-governing republic. Oaths of loyalty to the new political system became an important tool in helping sustain it.

In Article 2, cl. 8 of the U.S. Constitution requires the President to take an oath of office. Article 4, cl. 3 requires oaths of office for members of the U.S. Congress; the federal judiciary; and officers of state legislative, executive, and judicial branches of government. Loyalty oaths also played an important part in the naturalization process. Persons born in the United States are citizens by birth, but resident aliens who wish to become citizens must first swear an oath of allegiance to the United States.

During and after World Wars, the government enacted loyalty oaths for employees. Loyalty oaths have been regarded as essential tools in the defense of the United States from its enemies from both within and outside the country, this was especially true during wartime. Both during and after World War I and World War II, along with during the Cold War, widespread fear of communism, fascism, and socialism, and the concomitant anxiety of ensuring that Americans were and would remain loyal to the United States, led federal and state governments to enact legislation to weed out subversive organizations and those who supported them.

It was then that Congress aggressively investigated the loyalty of citizens, notably through the special House Un-American Activities Committee (HUAC) and the Senate Permanent Investigation Subcommittee. The HUAC enacted statutes, such as the Smith Act of 1940 and the 1950 McCarran Internal Security Act, which looked to increase the rise of communism in the United States. Both federal and state governments also enacted security programs that included loyalty oaths for government employees and members of labor unions and professional organizations.

The Pledge of Allegiance is a form of loyalty oath. State laws requiring students to salute the American flag and recite the Pledge of Allegiance in public schools led to the Supreme Court's landmark decision in West Virginia State Board of Education v. Barnette in 1943, which struck down West Virginia's mandatory flag salute statute as a violation of the First Amendment. The continued popularity of the Pledge of Allegiance as an avowal of patriotism is apparent in the ongoing conflict over its wording. However, not all loyalty oath cases are based on First Amendment.

The Supreme Court had decided many cases involving public employees' loyalty oaths, but not all were decided solely on First Amendment grounds. Some were based on due process rights, and others were based on the Fifth Amendment's privilege against self-incrimination. At one time, the Supreme Court first interpreted the constitutionality of loyalty oaths right after the Civil War, it declared them ex post facto laws and bills of attainder. Although the Court looked at 'clear and present danger' to government interest in considering loyalty oath.

In loyalty oath cases involving the First Amendment, the

government has been able to constitutionally require loyalty oaths of public employees, but the wording of the oath is all-important. The oath must specifically define and punish behavior that constitutes a clear and present danger to a substantial government interest. This includes not infringing on the First and Fourteenth Amendment right, along with an oath must not be so vague that those hearing it need to guess at its meaning. The oath must also not be a condition on employment or engage in activities where protected speech is taking place.

Chapter Sixteen

Test Oaths

I do solemnly swear that I will support and defend the Constitution of the United States against all enemies, foreign and domestic; that I will bear true faith and allegiance to the same; that I take this obligation freely, without any mental reservation or purpose of evasion; and that I will well and faithfully discharge the duties of the office on which I am about to enter. So help me God.

At the start of each new Congress, in January of every odd-numbered year, one-third of senators take an oath when beginning a new term into public office. While the oath-taking practice dates back to the First Congress in 1789, the current oath is a product of the 1860s, drafted during the Civil War.

The Constitution contains an oath of office for the president of the United States. For other officials, including members of Congress, that document specifies only that they "shall be bound by Oath or Affirmation to support this constitution." In 1789 the First Congress adopted a simple oath: "I do solemnly swear that I will support the Constitution of the United States."

At the outbreak of the Civil War in April of 1861, a time of an uncertain and shifting loyalties, President Abraham Lincoln ordered all federal civilian employees within the executive branch to take an expanded oath. After its emergency session that summer, Congress adopted legislation requiring executive branch employees to take the expanded oath in support of the Union. In July 1862 Congress added a new section to the oath, which became known as the "Ironclad Test Oath." The Test Oath required civilian and military officials to swear or affirm that they had never aided or encouraged "persons engaged in armed hostility" against the United States. Government employees who swore falsely would be prosecuted for perjury and forever denied federal employment. Congress also revised the rest of the oath with language that closely resembles the modern oath.

It wasn't until January 1864 where the Senate adopted a resolution that required all senators to take the Test Oath. The resolution also required senators to "subscribe" to the oath by signing a printed copy. This condition reflected a wartime practice in which military and civilian authorities required anyone wishing to do business with the federal government to sign a copy of the Test Oath. The current practice of newly sworn senators signing individual pages in an elegantly bound oath book dates from this period.

After the Civil War, Congress permitted some former Confederates to take only the second section of the 1862 oath, and an 1868 statute prescribed this alternative oath for "any person who has participated in the late rebellion, and from whom all legal disabilities arising therefrom have been removed by an act of Congress.

Northerners complained of the law's unfair double standard that required loyal Unionists to take the Test Oath's harsh first section while permitting ex-Confederates to ignore it. In 1884, after more than a decade of such complaints, a new generation of lawmakers repealed the first section of the Test Oath, leaving intact today's affirmation of constitutional allegiance.

A Test Oath is when someone is inaugurated to public office, he or she takes the "oath of office. It argues that no one should be permitted to hold public office who does not take a "test oath."

There are two definitions of "test oath" to be found in American legal history. The subject can be confusing because some court cases have used both definitions indiscriminately.

- An ordinary oath is a declaration that the oath-taker believes in God and that He will judge falsehood and broken promises.
- A "Test Oath" affirms further loyalty. In the past, this additional loyalty was to a king or a church.

Today, any oath which has an explicit reference to one's religious beliefs is often called a test oath. The history behind test oaths started in the middle Ages, kings, princes, and feudal lords demanded oaths of loyalty from their vassals. Not just to the prince, but to his religion as well. After the Reformation, if a prince became a Lutheran, everyone in his realm became a Lutheran. By law. Anyone accepting a political office or public trust took an oath of loyalty to the prince and to their faith.

In America, many of the colonies limited political offices to members of the Church of England, or other denominations. After the Revolution against Britain, very few people wanted their tax dollars to pay the salaries of the clergy for the Church of England (no surprise). But which denomination would be supported by taxes and oaths? The colonists decided to eliminate taxes and oaths which favored any particular denomination. Before the Constitution was written, every state had eliminated the requirement that public office holders be members of a particular denomination. The Revolution rather than the First Amendment effectively marked the end of test oaths and "established churches."

While every state still required that politicians believe in GOD. Non-believers could not take an oath. An oath was a declaration of belief in God. The oath taker declares that he believes in God and that he is fully aware that God will judge him if what he says is false or if what he promises is not fulfilled.

At the time the Constitution was ratified, these two points were universally understood:

- An oath could be taken only by someone who believed in God.
- An oath of office could be taken by anyone who believed in God, regardless of denominational affiliation. In short, no other "religious test" would be required.

Both before and after the Constitution was ratified, the states required candidates to be Biblically qualified to take the oath of office. They were not required to affirm their membership in a particular denomination, but they were required to swear that they were Christians. If you were not a Christian, you could not hold office.

As an example, see the Delaware Constitution, Art. 22 (adopted Sept. 20, 1776):

> Every person who shall be chosen a member of either house,
> or appointed to any office or place of trust . . .
> shall . . . make and subscribe the following declaration, to wit:
> "I ________, do profess faith in God the Father,
> and in Jesus Christ His only Son,
> and in the Holy Ghost, one God, Blessed for evermore;
> and I do acknowledge the Holy scripture
> of the Old and New, Testaments to be
> given by divine inspiration."

All states required Christian belief before the American Revolution. There was no other "religious test."
The U.S. Constitution banned "religious tests." Article VI, para. 3 reads:

> The Senators and Representatives before mentioned, and the members of the several state legislatures, and all executive and judicial officers, both of the United States and of the several states, shall be bound by oath or affirmation, to support this Constitution; but no religious test shall ever be required as a qualification to any office or

public trust under the United States.

At this point in time, the requirement of "an oath" was a requirement of an act of religious worship, a solemn declaration made in the presence of God. The option to "affirm" rather than "swear" was included for the benefit of Quakers, who would not take an oath, but did believe in God. The debates in the state ratifying conventions indicate that many Ratifiers understood the paragraph to be speaking of what might be called a "denominational" test.

No one would be required to be a member of a particular church/denomination. They assumed office-holders would be Christian. After drafting the Constitution, the Signers returned to their home states and drafted state constitutions that limited public office to Christians. In their minds, the Constitution did not change anything but merely protected what already existed.

Some scholars have argued that this provision applies only to Federal Offices, but not to state offices. In other words, the states would still be free to limit state offices to Episcopalians, if they so choose. However, the states had already ended this practice anyway. They didn't want the federal government to give privileges to who-knows-what denomination over the others.

On the other hand, the debates indicate some were concerned that an atheist could become President. In reply, men like Theophilus Parsons of Newburyport, MA, said Americans would *never* vote for an atheist, but an oath would be of no use because an atheist would simply lie or swear falsely that he was a Christian. The U.S. Supreme Court Justice Joseph Story, whose Commentaries on the Constitution were recognized as the most authoritative statement of the meaning of the Constitution, declared that as a result of this Article, "the Calvinist . . . and the Infidel may sit down at the common table of the national councils without any inquisition into their faith or mode of worship."

Today, Test Oaths no longer exist, since every form of oath is dead. Justice Story and other constitutional authorities have given secularists ammunition with which to attack the

Christian roots of our legal system. The doctrine of church and state took generations to construct. It is not found in the text of the Constitution. This is because of this doctrine, secularists today argue that any religious content at all in an oath is "unconstitutional." Secularists call the requirement that political of office holders believe in God a "test oath." But it was not until 1961 that the U.S. Supreme Court declared a requirement to believe in God unconstitutional. This led to the decision a few months later to ban prayer and Bible reading from the states' schools.

The Constitution does not require it, virtually every President since Washington has added the words "so help me, God" to his oath of office, indicating that they did not believe Article VI required completely secular oaths. But a strange thing has happened. A very strange thing. Although secularists were able to get "test oaths" declared unconstitutional in 1961, many legislatures and courts still require the use of the phrase "so help me, God" in all oaths. Atheists have gone to court on several occasions seeking to have this phrase eliminated.

They were logical to do so; the doctrine of the "separation of church and state" as articulated by the Supreme Court demands secular oaths. But courts were reluctant to face the adverse publicity such a decision would have. What they did was declare that the phrase "so help me, God" does not refer to God! One court said it had no theological purpose. However, without directly ruling on the issue, the U.S. Supreme Court has called the phrase "ceremonial deism." Back in the days of "test oaths," that same Court denounced as a form of *unbelief.* Many, many Christians have since taken an oath which the United States Supreme Court has defined as an acknowledgment that the oath taker would is an unbeliever. Christians must take steps to release themselves from these secular oaths and take a Christian "test oath." To do so would be to repudiate the entire edifice of secular church-state theory the courts have built over the years.

According to the U.S. Supreme Court, the oath is a formality today for those serving in public office, as predicted many years prior by George Washington. It "simply" requires the candidate to take a secular "oath" that he will "support the constitution" and perform his job "to the best of my ability." As a result, most people have sworn to "support the constitution" that they may not ever read before. Life and property are now threatened by the government, whose officers no longer have Godly reputations. It becomes necessary to restore the "test oath." Not out of loyalty to political parties, but rather as an allegiance to God.

Webster's 1828 edition of the *American Dictionary of the English Language* defines "oath" as follows:

A solemn affirmation or declaration, made with an appeal to God for the truth of what is affirmed. The appeal to God in an oath implies that the person imprecates His vengeance and renounces His favor if the declaration is false, or if the declaration is a promise, the person invokes the vengeance of God if he should fail to fulfill it. A false oath is called perjury.

Chapter Seventeen

Ai, Society, And Public Office

Artificial intelligence (AI) has many different definitions; some see it as the created technology that allows computers and machines to function intelligently. Some see it as the machine that replaces human labor to work for men a more effective and speedier result. Others see it as "a system" with the ability to correctly interpret external data, to learn from such data, and to use those learnings to achieve specific goals and tasks through flexible adaptation. Within the realm of politics, like many fields, there are concerns with the use of AI. In order to understand the effects that it has on politics, in particular oaths, recognizing the definition of AI is important to knowing how it will change public office and society as a whole.

Despite the different definitions, the common understanding of AI is that it is associated with machines and computers to help humankind solve problems and facilitate working processes. In short, it is an intelligence designed by humans and demonstrated by machines. The term AI is used to describe these functions of human-made tool that emulates the "cognitive" abilities of the natural intelligence of human minds.

According to the article, The Impact of artificial intelligence on human society and bioethics, there are different functions and abilities provided by AI, we can distinguish two different types.

The first is weak AI, also known as narrow AI that is designed to perform a narrow task, such as facial recognition or Internet Siri search or self-driving car. Many currently existing systems that claim to use "AI" are likely operating as a weak AI focusing on a narrowly defined specific function. Although this weak AI seems to be helpful to human living, there are still some think weak AI could be dangerous because weak AI could cause disruptions in the electric grid or may damage nuclear power plants when malfunctioned.

Strong AI is a different perception of AI that it can be programmed to actually be a human mind, to be intelligent in whatever it is commanded to attempt, even to have perception, beliefs and other cognitive capacities that are normally only ascribed to humans.

In summary, we can see these different functions of AI:

- Automation: Functioning automatically in society.
- Machine learning and vision: The science of getting a computer to act through deep learning to predict and analyze, and to see through a camera, analog-to-digital conversion, and digital signal processing.
- Natural language processing: The processing of human language by a computer program, such as spam detection and converting instantly a language to another to help humans communicate.
- Robotics: A field of engineering focusing on the design and manufacturing of cyborgs, the so-called machine man. They are used to perform tasks for human's convenience or something too difficult or dangerous for human to perform and can operate without stopping such as in assembly lines.
- Self-driving car: Use a combination of computer vision, image recognition amid deep learning to build automated control in a vehicle.

History tells us that human is always looking for something faster, easier, more effective, and convenient to finish the task they work on; therefore, the pressure for further development motivates humankind to look for a new and better way of doing things. Human society has been using the tools since the beginning of civilization, and human progress depends on it. Living in the 21st century did not have to work as hard as their forefathers in previous times because they have new machines to work for them.

Artificial intelligence (AI) has been beneficial for humanity, improving many human activities. However, there are now significant dangers that may increase when AI reaches a human level of intelligence or superintelligence. It is paramount to focus on ensuring that AI is designed in a manner that is robustly beneficial for humans. However, the ethics and personal responsibilities of AI in politics may play an important role in continuing the constructive use of AI in the future. Lessons can be learnt from the long and successful history of ethics. Therefore, a similar oath, such as the Hippocratic Oath, that includes AI for those in public office may increase awareness of the potential lethal threats of AI, enhance efforts to develop safe and beneficial AI to prevent corrupt practices and manipulations and invigorate ethical codes. The AI Public Office Oath would use a simple universal principle, one that focuses on the basis of human ethics, and in an analogous way, the proposed oath for AI could potentially enhance morality beyond consciousness and spread ethics across the universe.

Those in public office are all bound by a single, powerful commitment. Since there are many professions that have variations on this an ethical code of honor. Lawyers must privilege their clients. CEOs must value shareholders. Like these professions, AI technologies rely on the trust of clients. Most companies do not allow client auditing of their models for legitimate intellectual property reasons, and even if they did, very few people would have the technical knowledge to conduct such an assessment.

The proliferation of AI relies on an airtight relationship of trust, a shared understanding that AI must support the interests of the user and not interfere with them. Both technological, legal, and social safeguards must exist to build up this relationship of trust. The proliferation of AI relies on an airtight relationship of trust, a shared understanding that AI must support the interests of the user and not interfere with them. Both technological, legal, and social safeguards must exist to build up this relationship of trust, totalitarian versus pluralism in governing.

Technologies such as AI have the chance to spur a pluralist revival. The costs of totalitarian progressives and totalitarian conservatives are on full display across the world. Moreover, the potential for willing cooperation across global values and cultures means that many new opportunities are available for pluralists. Pluralism and truth are related. If there are many different factions around the world who don't work off of shared ideological assumptions, the easiest way to find common ground is to agree on fundamental scientific truths. Those who deny inconvenient scientific facts make it far more difficult to cooperate with the many factions who disagree with them.

Totalitarian factions of the right and left make up less than ten percent of Americans each. This is already a small minority in American terms, but in global terms, they make up less than half a percent. Imagine conforming the most powerful innovation in recent memory to the anti-scientific taboos of less than half a percent of people. Ultimately, it's a numbers game. Pluralists will win because, by the very nature of pluralism and totalitarianism, there are more of us than there are of them. The far-left and the far-right certainly won't work with each other. But the same is not true of the center-left, center, and center-right.

There is a strength in building a new type of Hippocratic Oath, one that would be used within public office. It is a truth about human trust across history. It doesn't require any existing ideology. It is familiar to anyone who has seen a doctor, visited a hospital, or taken medication. It is familiar to anyone who has needed a lawyer or bought a stock. It is the most basic building block of trust. Unlike totalitarians, pluralists are not motivated by the same extreme desires. We must return to basics and trust each other in order to build the coalitions necessary to defend ourselves, most importantly when it comes to the technology that will define the future.

Above all, we see the high-profile examples of AI including autonomous vehicles such as drones and self-driving cars, medical diagnosis, creating art, playing games, search engines such as Google searches, online assistants, image recognition in photographs, spam filtering, or predicting flight delays. All these have made human life much easier and convenient that we are so used to them and take them for granted. AI has become indispensable, although it is not absolutely needed for society to function. However, there is a negative impact that AI could have on us, including how it effects government, political campaigns, and elections.

Outside of public office, the progressive development of AI, human labor will no longer be needed, since everything would be able to be done mechanically. The process of evolution takes eons to develop, so we will not notice the backsliding of humankind. Here are some examples of how AI may affect human society.

1. A huge social change that disrupts the way we live in the human community. Society will become more industrious and will require people to be industrious in order to make a living. Human interaction will gradually diminish as AI will replace the need for people to meet face to face for idea exchange. AI will stand in between people as the personal gathering will no longer be needed, not even for communication.

2. Unemployment will be replaced by machinery. Today, many automobile assembly lines have been filled with machineries and robots, forcing traditional workers to lose their jobs. Even in supermarkets, the store clerks will not be needed anymore as the digital device can take over human labor.

3. Wealth inequality will be created as the investors of AI will take up the major share of the earnings. The gap between the rich and the poor will be widened.

4. Those who create AI may invent software that is racial bias or egocentrically oriented so to harm certain people or things. One instance is the United Nations, which has voted to limit the spread of nucleus power in fear of its indiscriminative use to destroying humankind or targeting on certain races or region to achieve the goal of domination. AI is possible to target certain races and could be destructed by programmers, and ultimately create world disasters.

From this perspective, we understand that AI can have a negative impact on humans and society; making it important to make sure that AI will not take off on its own by deviating from its originally designated purpose.

Stephen Hawking warned early in 2014 that the development of full AI could spell the end of the human race. He said that once humans develop AI, it may take off on its own and redesign itself at an ever-increasing rate. Intelligent AI can exhibit convergent behavior such as acquiring resources or protecting itself from being shut down, and it might harm humanity.

AI can reflect the very prejudices humans have tried to overcome. As AI becomes "truly ubiquitous," it has a tremendous potential to positively impact all manner of life, from industry to employment to health care and even security. Addressing the risks associated with the technology, The High-Level Expert Group on AI of the European Union presented Ethics Guidelines for Trustworthy AI in 2019 that suggested AI systems must be accountable, explainable, and unbiased. Three emphases are given:

1. Lawful-respecting all applicable laws and regulations.
2. Ethical-respecting ethical principles and values.
3. Robust-being adaptive, reliable, fair, and trustworthy from a technical perspective while taking into account its social environment.

There are six requirements are recommended:

1. AI should not trample on human autonomy. People should not be manipulated or coerced by AI systems, and humans should be able to intervene or oversee every software decision that is made.
2. AI should be secure and accurate. It should not be easily compromised by external attacks, and it should be reasonably reliable.
3. Personal data collected by AI systems should be secure and private, this includes with voting. It should not be accessible to just anyone, and it should not be easily stolen.
4. Data and algorithms used to create an AI system should be accessible, and the decisions made by the software should be "understood and traced by human beings." In other words, operators should be able to explain the decisions made by an AI system.
5. Services provided by AI should be available to all, regardless of age, gender, race, or other characteristics. Similarly, systems should not be biased along these lines.
6. AI systems should be auditable and covered by existing protections for whistleblowers. The negative impacts of systems should be acknowledged and reported in advance.

From these guidelines, we can suggest that future AI must be equipped with human sensibility or "AI humanities." To accomplish this, AI creators need to keep in mind that technology is to serve not to manipulate humans and society. A guiding principle would need to be established to help decrease unfair and unethical practices from taking hold of those in public office. Developing principles that help guide the future development of the AI technology. We must pay close attention on how it effects humans. This is because AI has been designed and manufactured by humans. Here are four principles to consider:

1. Beneficence: Beneficence means doing what is good for the people. AI should benefit the whole human

life, the society, and the universe.

2. Value-upholding: This refers to AI's congruence to social values, in other words, universal values that govern the order of the natural world must be observed.
3. Lucidity: AI must be transparent without hiding any secret agenda. It has to be easily comprehensible, detectable, incorruptible, and perceivable. AI technology should be made available for public auditing, in testing and review, and subject to accountability standards.
4. Accountability: AI creators must carry a heavy on the outcome and impact of AI on whole human society and the universe. They must be accountable for whatever they manufacture and create.

Although these principles and the discussion of AI may not seem relevant to its use of those in public office. The way that AI is used in society directly effects how those looking to serve and already do serve in public office by becoming mindful as to how AI can be used in electoral practices, in reaching people, and how information is delivered in the future.

Establishing procedures that includes AI is necessary. Politics requires that an oath of office exist. It requires the inclusion of AI in order to decrease the risk of unethical behavior. A new Hippocratic Oath that that represents a standard for those serving public office. Such an oath would look somewhat like this:

I will remember that there is art to being in public office as well as governing, and that honesty, transparency, and ethics may outweigh the politician's decision.

I will not be ashamed to say "I know not," nor will I fail to call in my colleagues when the skills of another are needed for a government's recovery.

I will respect the privacy of my constituents, for their concerns are not disclosed to me that the world may know. I will well and faithfully discharge the duties of the office on which I am about to enter and to fully understand the capabilities and limitations of the high-risk AI system as it effects my duties and the people.

Most especially must I tread with care in matters of life and of Liberty. If it is given me to help the people, all thanks. But it may also be within my power to consider all options to improve society; this awesome responsibility must be faced with great humbleness and awareness of my own frailty.

Above all, I must not play at God.

I will remember that I do not treat the Constitution, binding laws, or legislative practice and procedure without due diligence, where decisions may affect the person's family and economic stability. My responsibility includes these related problems, if I am to care adequately for the people.

I will prevent discourse whenever I can, for prevention is preferable to cure.

I will remember that I remain a member of society, with special obligations to all my fellow human beings, those sound of mind and body, as well as the infirm.

If I do not violate this oath, may I enjoy life and art, respected while I live and remembered with affection thereafter.

May I always act so as to preserve the finest traditions of my calling and may I long experience the joy of representing those who seek my help.

AI works according to an algorithm. It cannot empathize or have the ability to recognize good from evil. AI could make mistakes and so bridging the gap between human and material worlds becomes important to society and its effects on everyday life.

Chapter Eighteen

Faith In Public Office

Oaths of office are strangely ubiquitous in liberal-democratic regimes. They bind officeholders to their duties of office, but they do so by invoking divine or religious sanction for the performance of those duties. This divine witness to the oath of office appears to stand in as a guarantor of the political order, but it also looms large as an authority that is separate from, and in some sense stands above, the political order.

This opens up the possibility that this other sovereign may make moral demands that supersede those of the political order and the duties incumbent upon the office holder.

This is the paradox of the oath of office. It both guarantees the performance of official duties and subjects the content of those duties to external judgment. It is a paradox embedded in the very nature of the oath of office, which captures within its short compass the very large question of the relationship between religious conviction, moral principle, and political power.

Through a study of the use of oaths in our political systems. This includes their secular adaptation, the affirmation of office, much light can be shed on the nature of faith in public office and its Oaths.

Oaths of office come to us as vestiges of a previous age, or so it seems. They belong to a time when duty was before right and religious sanction was taken for granted.

During an era when the whole of morality turned on the discharge of one's moral duties, and the very foundation of justice was truth and fidelity to promises and agreements. Many countries such as Australia, treat oaths differently than the United States.

During an age when witnessed oaths cemented office-holders to the burdens of responsibility. Although despite this seeming distance from our own time, oaths and affirmations remain a ubiquitous presence in our public law and government administration. At her coronation ceremony the Queen promised under oath to govern the peoples of the United Kingdom and her overseas possessions according to their respective laws and customs; to cause law and justice, in mercy, to be executed in all her judgments; and to maintain the laws of God and the true profession of the gospel within the United Kingdom. The Governor-General promised under oath that he would be faithful and bear true allegiance to Her Majesty Queen Elizabeth the Second," and well and truly serve her Majesty ... in the office of Governor-General, and would do right to all manner of people after the laws and usages of the Commonwealth of Australia, without fear or favor, affection or ill will. All elected members of the Australian Parliament are required to swear or solemnly affirm their allegiance to the Queen, and the Prime Minister, Ministers, and Parliamentary Secretaries take an oath or affirmation of office and the executive counselor's oath or affirmation.

Justices of the High Court of Australia, like the judges of all Australian courts, are required to affirm or swear a similar oath of allegiance and service to the Queen and to promise to do right to all manner of people according to law without fear or favor, affection or ill-will. Witnesses in Australian courts are required to give evidence under oath or affirmation that the evidence they will give will be the truth, the whole truth, and nothing but the truth, and jurors are required to swear or affirm that they will give a true verdict according to the evidence.

Contemporary Australian law allows for affirmations instead of oaths, and statutory declarations instead of sworn affidavits in most circumstances, and oaths can now be taken in a manner consistent with the oath-taker's religion. Although these developments suggest a kind of "secularization" of Australian law and politics, it seems that the policy issues that arise today are more about accommodating religious diversity than they are about removing religion from public life.

The exact terms of the minister's oath of office have been changed five times in recent years: under Prime Ministers Paul Keating, John Howard, Kevin Rudd, Julia Gillard, and Tony Abbott; and the executive councilor's oath or affirmation was also changed under Prime Ministers Malcolm Fraser and Paul Keating. The main points of difference between these oaths and affirmations concerned whether the relevant promises were made to "the Queen," to "the Commonwealth of Australia," or to "the people of Australia."

If Australia had become a republic following the referendum in 1999, a new oath or affirmation would have been expected of the President and members of Parliament, requiring them to swear loyalty to the Commonwealth and the people.

The language of oaths is sometimes quite unusual to modern ears. In colonial New South Wales, each Justice of the Peace swore to "do equal right to the poor and the rich after my cunning, wit, and power, and after the laws and customs of the realm and statutes made thereof." This reflected the language of an oath required by Henry VIII in the thirty-fifth year of his reign, which called upon the swearer to promise with all of his "Body, Cunning, Wit, and uttermost … Power," and "without Guile, Fraud, or other undue Mean," that he would "observe, keep, maintain, and defend all of the King's Majesty's Stiles, Titles and Rights" with "the whole Effects and Contents of the Acts provided for the same, and all other Acts and Statutes made, or to be made, with this Realm," together with "the Derogation, Extirpation, and Extinguishment of the usurped and pretended Authority, Power, and Jurisdiction of the See and Bishop of Rome, and all other

Foreign Potentates."

Although they seem archaic throwbacks to a bygone era, oaths of office clearly matter. A person is not able to enter into public office and exercise official power until an appropriate oath or affirmation is duly made.

Chapter Nineteen

Acts Of Religion

An oath is an act of religion. Thomas Aquinas said that oaths were an act of latria or worship, the special reverence that is due to God alone. John Calvin called oaths a "species of divine worship," an act of "religious veneration." The Torah had thundered: "Thou shalt fear the LORD thy God, and serve him, and shalt swear by his name" (Deuteronomy 6:13). For, as the Letter to the Hebrews put it, "men swear 'y one greater than themselves, and with them, an oath given as confirmation is an end of every dispute" (6:16). The Qur'an warns: "those who exchange the covenant of Allah and their oaths for a small price will have no share in the Hereafter, and Allah will not speak to them or look at them on the Day of Resurrection, nor will He purify them, and they will have a painful punishment" (Sura 3:77). Although Jesus Christ countered all this when he said: "do not swear at all ... but let your 'Yes' be 'Yes', and your 'No', 'No'" (Matthew 5:33-37). Relying on this saying, the Quakers refused to take oaths at all, and there is a wonderful statement by Voltaire to the effect that the compact entered into by William Penn with his American neighbors was the only such treaty "that was not ratified by an oath, and was never infringed. Even the refusal of an oath was for the Quakers an act of religion.

Thomas Hobbes argued that an oath adds nothing to

obligations that already exist: a covenant, if lawful, binds the conscience with or without an oath; whereas an unlawful covenant is not binding even if confirmed by oath. Moses Mendelssohn, the great German philosopher of the Jewish Enlightenment, agreed that an oath adds nothing to the obligations that already exist, namely, the duty to tell the truth and to keep one's promises. The taking of an oath, he maintained, serves neither for a conscientious man nor for a determined profligate. The former already knows that God is a witness to everything he says and does; the latter has no conscience and will readily swear a false oath and lie. All that the oath does, he said, is to fortify the irresolute and wavering to those who have principles, but do not always live up to them.

Immanuel Kant said something similar. The oath, he argued, presumes that a man who is not disposed to tell the truth will nonetheless be persuaded to do so by calling divine punishment down upon himself, "just as though it rested upon him whether or not to render account to this supreme tribunal." The oath is a kind of "spiritual torture," Kant said, which might be justified pragmatically, but that is all. It would be better if we told the truth because it is simply the right thing to do. For such a people, no oath is needed.

Certainly, the abuse of oaths can be very great. Under the Weimar Constitution of 1919, members of the German military swore loyalty to the Reich Constitution and pledged obedience to it. After Adolf Hitler was appointed Chancellor in 1933, however, the oath of loyalty was reframed so that it was addressed to the People and the Fatherland, and when the offices of Chancellor and President were merged in 1934, it was further transformed into an oath of personal loyalty to Adolf Hitler himself – as Leader of the German Empire and People.

This personal oath of loyalty to the Fuhrer was required of civil servants and government officials, including university professors and church pastors. Karl Barth, the famous Professor of Theology, then at the University of Bonn, refused to take the oath unless it was clearly understood to be subject to his prior responsibilities to God as an Evangelical Christian. Without this qualification, he argued, a promise of unlimited obedience would treat Hitler as if he were some kind of "a god incarnate.

Under the extreme pressure of the time, however, the Confessing Church stated that because an oath involves an acknowledgment of God as a divine witness, it necessarily excludes "any actions which would be contrary to God's command attested in Holy Scripture." On this understanding, Barth decided he could take the oath, but he was nevertheless dismissed from his post at the University for raising the issue in the first place and was soon forced to leave the country. From his native Switzerland, he continued to question the loyalty oath as purporting to displace the unqualified loyalty owed by a Christian to the Lord Jesus Christ.

Dietrich Bonhoeffer, who was later killed for his courageous opposition to Nazism and his role in the attempt to assassinate Hitler, was not required to take the oath because he was already deemed an illegal pastor, but he attempted to convince his fellow pastors not to do so. For Bonhoeffer, "no earthly obligation is absolutely binding" and it was therefore illegitimate to take any oath which made an "unconditional demand" after the style of the Hitler oath.

Adolf Eichmann, an infamous SS Officer found guilty of crimes against humanity, war crimes, and crimes against the Jewish people for his role in the organization of the Holocaust, had no such scruples. At his trial, he infamously excused his behavior as the carrying out of orders. "I am guilty of having been obedient," he said, of "having subordinated myself to my official duties and the obligations of war service and my oath of allegiance and my oath of office." Hannah Arendt controversially perceived a "banality of evil" in Eichmann's wooden and obtuse responses to questioning, but Bettina Stangneth has recently argued that Eichmann was far from a mindless functionary, hardly have "a small cogged in Adolf Hitler's extermination machine" as he had maintained throughout his office.

Chapter Twenty

Dark Oaths

Dark oaths can also be conspiratorial and subversive. Tacitus records the promises extracted from the Batavian chiefs by the one-eyed Gaius Julius Civilis, who collected them "at a sacred grove under the pretext of giving a banquet," persuaded them to join his revolt, and then "bound them all by their national forms of oath and barbarous rites." Rembrandt depicts the scene memorably in his dark, grotesque, and mordant Conspiracy of Claudius Civilis (1661-62). Members of the city council of Amsterdam, who had commissioned the painting to celebrate the construction of their new town hall, seem not to have been amused.

Life and death. Judgment of the body in this life and the soul in the hereafter. It is difficult to overestimate the significance of the oath. Was Jacques Derrida exaggerating when he said that the oath makes a promise that human language cannot undo? In the Merchant of Venice, Shylock regarded himself as bound by his oath to perform his promise to extract a proverbial pound of flesh from Antonio upon default of that infamous loan. Commenting on the binding power of the oath, Derrida wrote:
"The oath, the sworn faith, the act of swearing is transcendence itself, the experience of passing beyond man, the origin of the divine or if one prefers, the divine origin of the oath."

Carl Schmitt is famous for the claim that all of the important ideas in our modern liberal politics are secularized theological concepts. Schmidt had the idea of sovereignty, especially in mind, but he might just as easily have been talking about the oath and the solemn affirmation. Derrida suggested just this when he observed that even when God is not named, that is, even in the most secular pledge of commitment, His Presence is nonetheless implicitly invoked.

Charles Barbour, following Derrida, locates within our language and communication a whole array of theological concepts that haunt our ostensibly secular modernity. All social, political, and legal relations, he argues, are structured by something like an oath, a mutual promise to trust each other's word. The problem that the oath addresses concerns what he calls "the opacity of the other" – the mundane fact that we cannot know what another is thinking and must therefore accept their promises on trust. Our reliance on oaths and solemn affirmations is testimony to the faith that we must invest in each other, especially those who rule over us. It was not necessary to venture too deeply into the labyrinth of post-modern philosophy to see the point. An implied promise of fidelity is presupposed by human communication. Oaths of office propose to externalize and formalize this act of faith. In so doing, they purport to domesticate what has been called that wild or vast notion of what in every man's conception is just or unjust.

PART V

Chapter Twenty-One

Locations Of Sovereignty

Oaths and affirmations of office track the ebb and flow of ultimate authority and binding power within societies and cultures. They simultaneously reveal the location of our highest religious commitments and the grounds upon which the coercive powers of government are exercised.

The ancient civilizations of the Mediterranean basin Babylon, Egypt, Assyria, Greece, Rome, and many others were related to each other through treaty covenants sworn before their respective gods.

Many of these treaty covenants, were not agreements among equals but were rather the terms of a hegemonic relationship between suzerain and vassal. As scholars such as Peter Karavites and Moshe Weinfeld have shown, although the specific terms and rituals differed from one culture to another, the structural similarities point to a common origin and a shared set of understandings about the role of oaths in binding kings and nations to their obligations. Under conditions of polytheism, the gods of all the relevant nations were invoked as witnesses to the treaties.

The practice of confirming international treaties with an oath continued after the Christianization of the Roman Empire but was based on a shared monotheism. It was not until some point after the Enlightenment that this practice came to an end. As Allen Hertz has pointed out, thereafter the binding force of international treaties had to depend upon a natural law obligation to keep one's promises, or else the geo-political self-interest of states and the threat of military intervention.

The Germanic peoples of Europe placed a great deal of emphasis on the oath. A person charged with wrongdoing could rebut the charge by swearing an oath of innocence. It might also be determined that a person charged with a debt must prove his innocence with the assistance of twelve or more oath-helpers who would swear to their belief in the defendant's oath.

The reasons for the decline in this practice, which was called canonical purgation in ecclesiastical courts and wager of law in the common law courts – are complicated and obscure. It made some sense in local communities where personal reputation as a real constraint on behavior, as well as a means by which the secret sexual sins of clergy and accusations of adultery might be addressed within ecclesiastical law, but these considerations did not apply to the common law administered by the royal courts at Westminster. Over time, compurgation was displaced by trial by jury and the testimonial oath, which had been institutionalized in Roman jurisprudence as early as Emperor Constantine, who erroneously believed he was following Christian practice by requiring witness statements to be sworn on oath.

Oaths were certainly a mainstay of medieval civilization. One only has to list them: oaths of homage and allegiance, oaths of chivalry, oaths of fraternity, vows of pilgrimage, chastity, or celibacy, oaths of jurors and office-holders. The emergent towns and cities of medieval Europe, Harold Berman observes, were "religious associations in the sense that each was held together by religious values and rituals, including religious oaths." The charters by which the cities were established were "confirmed by religious oaths, and the oaths, which were renewed with successive installations of officers, included, above all, vows to uphold the municipal laws."

The oath-bound confederation was a common institution of medieval Europe where the rise of social contract theory – the idea that state authority is based on an agreement among the people – cannot be understood apart from this context. However, it was oaths of a rather different kind – oaths of fealty, allegiance, and abjuration – which came into their own as tools of European statecraft during the tumultuous sixteenth and seventeenth centuries.

To imagine a ruler succeeding to the throne based on a solemn oath was very consistent with the Reformation insistence on the importance of secular vocations, through which every layman was called directly into the service of God. But in the hands of Henry VIII, the oath of allegiance functioned as a potent means of maintaining control over his subjects. As Thea Cervone pointed out: rather than describing fealty to the monarch, Henry VIII wished for the Oaths of Supremacy and Succession to describe fealty to him." Another observed: "The Tudor state had succeeded to the church's role as arbiter of the individual conscience and then set about investing loyalty oaths with obligations arising from conscience.

A multitude of oaths and subscriptions were used by Henry VIII to secure his new divorce, the succession of the throne, and his supremacy over the English church. One only has to mention the oaths associated with Henry VIII's Act of Succession in 1534 and Elizabeth I's later Act of Supremacy, and James I's Popish Recusants Act to recognize the significance of the oath in Tudor and Stuart statecraft.

Elizabeth I had a supremacy oath was required of every archbishop, bishop, and all and every other ecclesiastical person and "every temporal judge, justice, mayor, and other lay or temporal officer and minister. Under the oath, the promisor was required to declare that the queen was "the only supreme governor" over the realm and all her majesty's overseas dominions, not only in temporal affairs, but also in all spiritual or ecclesiastical matters. The oath-taker was also required to swear that "no foreign prince, person, prelate, state or potentate has, or ought to have" any jurisdiction within the realm, and had to "utterly renounce and forsake all foreign jurisdictions, powers, superiorities, and authorities."

James, I had an oath of allegiance that further required the swearer to deny the power of the pope to depose the king or authorize armed rebellion against him, and to deny any such effect to any sentence of ex-communication of the king. Sir Thomas More and Bishop John Fisher were executed precisely because they refused to take Henry VIII's oath of succession, particularly as it required the oath-taker to abjure "any foreign potentate," which was to impugn the authority of the pope in favor of the king.

The oath, says one scholar, thus became an irresistibly attractive tool of the authorities. For it is a powerful, infrangible, obligation that can bind the individual to the big political entities, the nation, and the national church.

William Shakespeare well recognized this, as the pivotal role of oaths, vows, and conscriptions in his many plays attests. Now oaths are so frequent, since the mid-seventeenth century, they should be taken like pills, swallowed whole: if you chew them you will find them bitter: if you think of what you swear, twill hardly go down.

The ex officio oath which required defendants to swear to answer questions even if their answers might incriminate them was a particularly useful tool in the hands of the Star Chamber and High Commission.

It was a procedure whereby a charge of heresy could be pursued even where there were no independent witnesses when the defendant was accused instead by clamosa insinuatio that is by 'public scandal'. In such a case the judge or ordinary was empowered to act ex officio and to ask the accused to take an oath to answer truthfully and absolutely any question that was asked of him. There was no specific bill of charges, no indictment providing the limits of allowable questioning. There was also no legal counsel for the accused. The judge effectively took the part also of prosecution and even of defense. The odds against the accused in such circumstances were catastrophic. Unless he was himself an expert in theology, he was virtually certain to convict himself of some heresy or other under such open rules of examination.

William Tyndale, like many Protestant reformers who followed him, objected to the use of state power to inquire into the private beliefs and thoughts in this way. He argued that judgment ought to proceed only based on evidence sworn by witnesses, and should not presume to inquire into men's consciences:

> "in the causes that are brought to them, when they sit in God's stead, let them judge and condemn the trespasser under lawful witnesses ... Let what is known only to God, and of which no proof can be made or lawful witness brought, abide until the coming of the Lord, who will reveal all secrets ... God has given them no further authority."

The Star Chamber and High Commission were abolished by the Habeas Corpus Act and High Commission Abolition Act, and the erection of such courts was denounced by the Bill of Rights as being illegal and pernicious. The privilege against self-incrimination enjoyed by defendants today is largely a result of the common law's reaction against the use of the ex officio oath.

Oaths of office and oaths of allegiance have been the example of state authority. They have determined its metes and bounds, and continue to do so. During the English civil war, publicists of all perspectives found it necessary to address the question of the oath as a way of identifying the proper bounds of the authority of the king, the parliament, and the people.

James I had maintained that only God could enforce the coronation oath against the king, and Philip Hunton argued that the people continue to owe obedience to the king under their oaths of subjection. On the other hand, Samuel Rutherford insisted that if the "oath betwixt the king and his people" is broken, "the party injured is loosed from the contract" and the people operating through their inferior magistrates may resist tyranny on the part of the king.

Anthony Ascham, like Thomas Hobbes, later argued that self-preservation is the most basic obligation so that no oath could oblige the oath taker to comply with his oath if that should prejudice his own safety and that the oath binds him no more than he intended to be bound when taking the oath. However, Robert Sanderson, who was chaplain to Charles I, responded that this would tend, among other things:

> "To the bringing in of atheism, with the contempt of God and all religion, whilst every man, by making his preservation the measure of all his duties and actions, makes himself thereby his own idol."

The sentence of Oliver Cromwell's High Court of Justice, which convicted Charles I of high treason, was premised specifically on the "trust, oath, and office" committed to him – to be used, it was said, for the "good of the people" and for the "preservation of their liberties," and not to erect in himself an "unlimited and tyrannical power to rule according to his will." While those involved in the trial and execution of the king were later themselves executed for regicide and the breach of their own duties of loyalty, the assertion of the Parliament's ultimate control over the terms of the coronation oath, the succession to the Crown and the oath of allegiance were crucial to the establishment of its sovereignty as a result of the "glorious revolution" of 1688-1689. Thus were established the constitutional assumptions of Australian law and government.

Chapter Twenty-Two

Allegiance And Sovereignty

In more recent times, in Australia, differing views about the nature and location of sovereignty have been at the heart of changes to the oaths of office and oaths of allegiance required of our public officials. However, sovereignty is a notoriously ambiguous and contested concept. For a start: is it vested in the Queen, the Parliament, or the Australian people? The constitutional answer to this question is far from clear, and the terms of the oaths and affirmations of office within the various Australian jurisdictions reflect this ambiguity. And what is the role and status of our judges in this context? One may have to ask whether today's judges, exercising vast powers of judicial review over legislation and executive action, are always faithful to their oath-bound obligation to do justice "according to law."

Sir Gerard Brennan had occasion on his swearing-in as Chief Justice of the High Court of Australia to reflect on the judicial oath as the ground upon which he was obliged to do justice according to law and not according to his own view of what the law ought to be, which was "that wild or vast notion of what in every man's conception is just or unjust."

Paolo Prodi has argued that "the early modern state's monopolization of oaths represents a socialization of power in the first step towards a 'secular oath'." In this connection, it may be worth recalling Dietrich Bonhoeffer's observation that there are two ways in which untruthfulness can undermine an oath: "either it may actually insinuate itself into the oath, or else disguise itself in the form of an oath by invoking some secular or divine power instead of the living God."

The religious oath may be a ready tool in the hands of the political authorities from Henry VIII to Adolf Hitler – but its complete secularization can also mark a shift toward totalitarianism. The Soviet Union had an oath, but it was an oath that invoked not God, but rather the "stern punishment of Soviet law" and the "universal hatred and contempt" of the proletariat. Joseph Stalin promulgated the following oath of allegiance for members of the Red Army:

> "I, a citizen of the Union of Soviet Socialist Republics, joining the ranks of the Workers' and Peasants' Red Army, do hereby take the oath of allegiance and do solemnly vow to be an honest, brave, disciplined and vigilant fighter, to guard strictly all military and State secrets, to obey implicitly all Army regulations and orders of my commanders, commissars, and superiors … And if through evil intent I break this solemn oath, then let the stern punishment of the Soviet law, and the universal hatred and contempt of the working people, fall upon me."

Aleksandra Solzhenitsyn testified to what the stern punishment of Soviet law looked like in practice. In his accounts of Soviet justice, there is very little reference to the sworn testimony of witnesses, and much more about endless interrogations, exquisite tortures, and forced confessions.

An oath may be a kind of spiritual torture, as Kant said, but it respects the internal domain of a person's conscience as something known and judged by God alone. In a review of Giorgio Agamben's The Sacrament of Language: An Archaeology of the Oath, Justin Clemens observes:

> "It is thus no wonder today, when the oath has

> fallen into desuetude that torture is explicitly back on the agenda even for those democratic states which had prided themselves on their thoroughgoing rejection of it. Without any trust in oaths – indeed, having repudiated almost altogether their function and efficacy – our contemporary materialist polities can imagine no other recourse than direct psycho-physical incursions into bodies in a forlorn and terrifying attempt to extract 'reliable' 'information'."

If this is so, the advice given to early Anglo-Saxon kings by Dunstan, Archbishop of Canterbury believed that may have been worth recalling, as he said:

> "The justice of a consecrated king is that he condemns no man [unjustly]; and that he defend and protect widows and orphans and foreigners; …have the old and wise and temperate as his counsellors, and appoint righteous men as officers; because, whatever they do unjustly by means of his might, he must give a reckoning on judgment day for all of it."

The Code of Emperor Justinian spoke in a similar register when requiring that judges must not "permit the hearing of a process to begin unless there is a copy of the Holy Scriptures placed before the judicial bench." It was observed that:

> "Attending in this way to the holy Scriptures and consecrated by the presence of God, they will have greater assistance in their decisions from the knowledge that they are as much judged as judging, and that judgment is more terrible for them than for the parties, since the weighing of a litigant's cause is a matter for man's supervision, the weighing of a judge's cause is reserved for God's." In good conscience, politicians cannot overlook the Oath.

Overlooking the oath, or not recognizing it as problematic,

above all because it was a religious act, has been a remarkably economical way of creating a premature secularization of political debate in which issues of office then need to be pared down to suitably secular politics, of promises and agreements and contractual rights, to conform to expectations.

There has, undoubtedly, been a Richard S. Willen, 'Rationalization of Anglo-Legal Culture: The Testimonial Oath.' The British Journal of Sociology" Secularization in our practice of oaths and affirmations. But we have to be careful about what we mean by secularization. The solemn affirmation as a substitute for the oath was originally invented for religious reasons to avoid injury to the religious consciences of Anabaptists, Quakers, and Moravians.

Even today, a clear majority of our officeholders still opt for the religious oath. Since the late 1970s, a fairly consistent figure of around 70% of senators and 75% of members of the House of Representatives have chosen to take oaths rather than solemn affirmations. And even in the most secular of states the Soviet Union a secular oath was still found to be indispensable. The chilling thing is that as fearful as the judgment of God might be, the horrors that Solzhenitsyn recounted in his Gulag Archipelago were enough of hell upon the earth as it is.

The oath of office places a limit on public power. It binds our governors to the responsibilities of the office and reminds them that they are as much judged as judging. The oath suggests that if we are to have faith in public office, we will also need to keep faith in public office.

Chapter Twenty-Three

Ethical Standards

Setting the bar that holds politics are its representatives to hold themselves to ethics is an important first step to being effective in government. Having to separate politics from the government has not been an easy task for many in public office. Holding to a reputation that there are no strings attached to making decisions for their communities, there is no room to carry themselves without a strong sense of ethics.

Stressing the importance of open government and keeping information available to the public are ways that political reformers have kept a high standard of ethics. Having little reporting efforts by the media has contributed to too many local governments becoming corrupt. The advancement of technology allows for greater transparency and accountability to become a realistic goal for politicians. With the development of the World Wide Web, which began in Geneva in March 1989, when a written proposal for an Internet framework would allow online documents to link to one another. Often parallel, the World Wide Web and the movement towards accountability and transparency have become increasing in interest.

Transparency is a medium in which the way that we view things and how others view us. The belief is that more transparency increases accountability; along with published information. However, a new directive requiring stricter documentation of government meetings led to an increase in "informal lunches" where public officials can discuss topics without making their discussions publicly accessible. Such behavior could lead many to believe that public officials are discussing secrets they wish to hide from the public. Other types of technology such as social media allow for information to be shared between politicians and the people. Social media is no longer a new medium. Instead, it has become the norm for communication. Providing solutions to encourage the people to become involved in government, the idea behind transparency is to improve engagement. It is a matter of understanding the needs of the people first before building policies.

For political reformers, holding such events as mandatory ethics training to all department and senior staff is important to maintain trust in government. Pieces of training such as "The Quest for Government Integrity" seminar are provided with the intention that as public officials, they share the sacred trust of public service. Administrations should be expected to fulfill such training before becoming government employees or appointed officials. This is one way to uphold trust, with the thinking that presenting such a seminar would be another way to educate city employees on the laws about local government, with Open, honest, and transparent government. This is what was pledged during his campaign. One way to achieve it was by providing ethics training as an important step in ensuring that city employees were educated and on notice about the penalties for violating ethics laws.

These were just some of the principles that are faced in political reform and governing. It's the ability to move a community forward. Over the past ten years, we are seeing a greater need for reforms to be developed. Congress has failed in recent years to enact a reform making children safer from gun violence. However, many in politics have put in place a bid specification to purchase new weaponry, with police departments become the majority of buyers of guns and ammunition. It was the first policy to bring about a needed expectation of what gun manufacturers owed the people when it came to their safety. As part of the policy, the government is beginning to ask all bidders the following six socially responsible questions:

- What do you do to combat illegal gun trafficking and illegal gun crime?
- Do you manufacture and sell assault weapons for civilian use?
- Do you agree not to sell certain models of firearms for civilian use?
- Are you requiring your dealers to conduct background checks?
- Do you fund research related to gun violence and smart gun technology?
- Will you commit to prohibiting your brand name from being used in violent video games?

With much skepticism, especially among gun manufactures, ethics plays a role in decision-making. Political reformers will look for opportunities to pay it forward for the people in their communities. By taking a stand on issues such as gun reform, many realize that their communities could become a little safer. The hope was that more cities and state governments would soon follow and stand boldly for the people. This is the overall thinking of a political reformer.

Chapter Twenty-Four

The Political Salesman

Political candidates and political parties have become increasingly thinking of ways to market themselves, and it is becoming an integral part of politics. Political marketing is a global phenomenon with political parties are basing their campaigns and their public image on the results of marketing research. A central issue in the broader marketing discipline is the tension interactions between salespeople and marketing, rather than the assumed fit between these domains. The emergence of these tensions can be found in the political domain that is causing an increase in a political civil war, where salesmanship becomes vastly more of an interest when working in public office. In many ways, politicians have become project leaders in the big business of legislating.

Politicians are in many ways like project leaders of public office, where they should consider the environment within which their decisions will take place. They should consider how decisions are taken within and about their work, this includes their promises, where their decision-making is located in one of two worlds: the world of the sales representative and the world of the politician. In the end, a politician is much like a salesman.

The world of the sales representative revolves around profit maximization, and stability is very important. Actions are based on mutual trust and are subject to the motto of, a deal is a deal. Relationships among sales representatives are important, and the behavior that they exhibit is genuine and power becomes decentralized.

In the world of the politician, the majority is important for getting things done. Loyalty to the group is thus important, even if a politician's opinion differs from that of the group on many points. Because the majority seldom consists of a single group, temporary coalitions are often necessary, sometimes with opponents or even enemies. Decisions emerge from a particular view of the world. In the world of the politician, references to certain facts are necessary to maintain good order; the end justifies the means, and where power can be centralized.

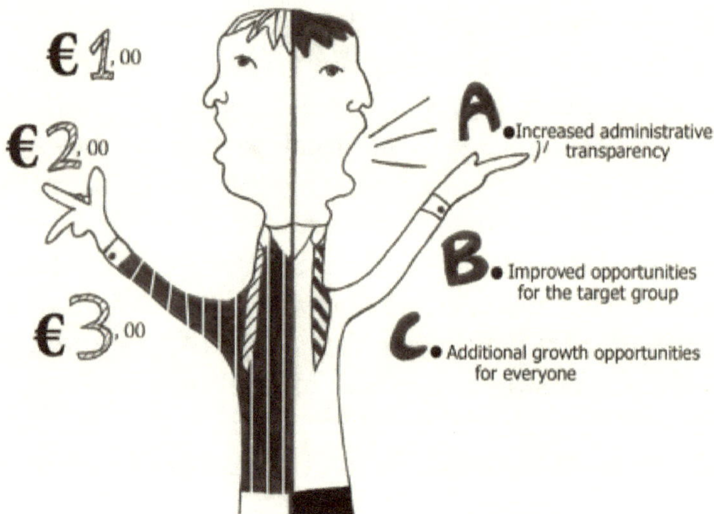

The sales representative and the politician

Although, most people find the world of the sales representative the more attractive of the two, it has an important disadvantage. Decision-making according to profit maximization works only for decisions in which clear cash flows are available. Decisions that involve such dilemmas or issues as investing more in education, the environment, health care, highways, research, defense, or nuclear energy cannot be expressed as an unambiguous balance between profit and loss. The political model is the only possible model for such decisions. It is therefore necessary to play the political game.

By definition, social and subsidized organizations exist within the world of the politician. The financing of these organizations and their projects are completely or largely dependent upon the political will to support the organization. The effectiveness of social organizations is not easily expressed in terms of cash flows. This is also true of the results of projects that are carried out by social organizations.

A young engineer once had to carry out an ambitious wind-energy project in a municipality somewhere in the country. Through an ingenious savings system, residents of the municipality could save for several windmills, to generate thirty percent of the town's electricity needs with their windmills. This would require ten windmills. The idea originated with one of the members of the town council.

The townspeople were considerably less enthusiastic about the savings programmer than had been expected. With great difficulty, they were able to save enough to purchase one-half of a windmill. To prevent the idea from becoming a complete failure, the municipality decided to supplement the amount, so that at least one windmill could be installed.

In the first draft of the final report, the engineer wrote that the result was quite disappointing. Such a report, however, would mean loss of face for the council member, who therefore urged a reformulation. The text ultimately came to read as follows: The project is a great success; the municipality has demonstrated its support for the environment and has made it is however a modest contribution to the fight against climate change. The young engineer was initially unaware of the political framework of this project. To prevent future projects from the council member from getting off the ground, he was forced to play, along with politics.

It is more difficult to carry out a project in a political environment than it is to carry one out in the environment of the sales representative. Decisions surrounding a project depend upon the political game and not on what would be most effective for the project. The catalyst for beginning a project is often political, and it, therefore, determines the force fields with which the project team is confronted.

Because of a reorganization, several organizations needed to merge and cooperate. This re-organization was mandated from above and involved, among other things, replacing several small-town local affiliates with a central office in the region. This meant that employees would have to travel much farther to their work. The work itself changed as well; many fewer positions for highly educated workers were available after the re-organization. A portion of the personnel had to seek positions outside of the organization or to other positions that were substantively much less interesting. There was therefore considerable resistance to the re-organization, even though it would mean considerable improvement in service for the customers if it proved successful. Finally, the re-organization was to be carried by the personnel themselves, under the supervision of a project leader.

The project leader initially had difficulty getting the project started. The team members who were to carry out the work kept finding excuses not to do their jobs. There was always a problem or setback, and there was considerable discussion. The discussions usually shifted to the question of whether the project itself was a good idea. The project leader would then defend the project it would mean a great improvement for the customers but he was unable to generate any enthusiasm for the project.

Once the project leader realized that many of the workers did not fully support the project, he decided to focus first on the task of reducing resistance to the project. He accomplished this by taking the time to visit the various affiliates. He also talked more with the supervisors and employees, often informally at the coffee machine. By developing a better relationship with a number of the formal and informal power-holders, he was able to kick-start the project when it faltered. The project remained difficult, but the political approach worked much better than had the rational approach that he had tried initially. A guide for playing politics would exceed this approach since the political game often takes place at the level of relationships and power relations. In a business environment, the product itself is more in the foreground.

Project leaders should realize that projects that are carried out with social organizations always involve at least some element of politics. To make projects successful, project leaders in this situation would be wise not to detach themselves from the political game. Instead, they should seek to play it as well as possible while providing substantive direction to their projects. More importantly, the game of salesmanship has changed the landscape of politics, and instead, the players involved have caused a civil war, a war game of broken promises that many outside of politics believe to be true. This is how the civil war of the political salesman continues, as a new race emerges between Democrats and Republicans.

Chapter Twenty-Five

Oath Keepers

A new race would need to emerge for both Democrats and Republicans alike in the United States. It is crucial to find political candidates that embrace fresh ideas and the ability to improve the welfare of the people. In states where credit ratings have been dropped by Moody, political reform is a concern when looking at politics and government. With some longtime politicians being projected to run for public office over the next few years, it becomes imminent to find political reformers. With many key Democrats and Republicans putting their hope in their candidates to run and to win, one fact remains, many have tried a run for public office and have failed.

The focus and attention on the people are to ultimately be at the forefront of any candidate's plans for the future. Examples of past political campaigns, such as Hillary Rodham Clinton, who lost the 2016 presidential campaign to Donald Trump, and the decline of Jeb Bush to win the GOP nomination. From 1992 to 2008, Green Party candidate Ralph Nader ran for the presidency and lost every time. But many have accused him of changing the course of the 2000 election and accused him of taking away several key swing states from Al Gore, costing him the election.

In 1992, Texas billionaire Ross Perot shocked the political system while running as an Independent Party candidate against

Democrat Bill Clinton and Republican George H.W. Bush. The businessman would go on to become the most successful third-party candidate in the history of American politics. His campaign took a strange turn when he dropped out of the race during the height of his popularity, but he later re-emerged weeks before the election and managed to gain 19 percent of the popular vote.

Aligning with some of the best political consultants and holding to a succession of fundraising money has been shown to not be enough for political candidates. An extra impediment for political candidates is their long-standing reputation for being a hotbed of political corruption. Many have been viewed by the people and the media for the end of their political career, was seen as being sort of grubby and corrupt.

Throughout the projections as to the next election, political reformers continue to be engaged in trash pickup, recycling, policing, the fire department structure, healthy living, revamping the 911 system; along with the many challenges that the people and their communities face.

There are factors to consider with regards to the projections that a political reformer could take a chance and run in an election and win. For instance, a resume of military service, work experience in finance, prior years working in government or corporate America, and the belief that the American Dream can still exist. With national security being a concern, along with both a crime rate and poverty levels increasing, there may be challenges to being elected, even as a reformer. Although political reformers can make a positive impact, there is still an unforgiving nature when it comes to voting. This is unfortunately true when looking at religion and culture. For the local government, it works, unfortunately, at a state or national level, the idea falls short. It by no means is a true indication as to his abilities to hold the position. The truth is, our government system has been filled by the "old school political machine," a machine that many desires to no longer exist, as the people have spent years trying to defeat it.

The positive effects of political reformers and their journeys haven't been lasting ones only for them, but instead, it has promoted an image of what a politician can have to allow them to succeed over decades. A candidate that can bring promise, hope, and positive change to a people. In the words of the Marine motto, a reformer that will leave no man or woman behind as their solemn vow. To end the Civil War of corruption in politics and to create a hierarchy that diminishes the political salesman means using a Lincoln leadership of governing. It would also mean being oath keepers in public office, so that we can build a perfect union between government and the people.

In the end, it's not the years in your life that count.

It's the life in your years. — Abraham Lincoln

References

Bianco, W. T., and Canon, D. T. *Chapter 6. The Media.* American Politics Today. Retrieved from the World Wide Web: http://www.wwnorton.com/college/polisci/american-politics-today3/full/ch/06/outline.aspx

Campaign for Political Reform (n.d.). A Global Initiative for Political Reforms. Retrieved from the World Wide Web: http://politicalreforms.org/meaning_of_political_reform.html

Ferrell, R.H. (n.d.) Eisenhower Was a Democrat. Retrieved May 12, 2016, from the World Wide Web: https://www.kshs.org/publicat/history/1990autumn_ferrell.pdf

FTI Journal. (2013). Social vs. Traditional Media. Retrieved from the World Wide Web: http://www.ftijournal.com/article/social-vs-traditional-media

Fleming, T. "I Am the Law." *American Heritage* June 1969: 32-48.

Goodwin, D. (2006). Team of Rivals: The Political Rivals of Abraham Lincoln. Simon & Schuster, New York.

Hausman, A. (2012). Major Differences between Social Media and Traditional Media. Retrieved from the World Wide Web: http://www.business2community.com/social-media/16-differences-between-social-media-and-traditional-media-0211995

Miller Center, University of Virginia, (2015). American Presidents: A Reference Source, Abraham Lincoln. Retrieved from the World Wide Web: http://millercenter.org/president/lincoln/essays/biography/3

Pew Research Center, (2020). Five Facts about Partisan Reactions to COVID-19 in the U.S. Retrieved from the World Wide Web: www.pewresearch.org

Pew Research Center, (2014). Public Trust in Government: 1958-2014. Retrieved from the World Wide Web: http://www.people-press.org/2014/11/13/public-trust-in-government/

Schambra, W. A. and West, T. (2007). The Progressive

Movement and the Transformation of American Politics. Retrieved from the World Wide Web: http://www.heritage.org/political-process/report/the-progressive-movement-and-the-transformation-american-politics

The White House, (2009). Ethics. Retrieved from the World Wide Web: http://www.whitehouse.gov/issues/ethics/

Turner, M., (1998). The Literary Mind. Oxford University Press; Revised ed. Edition.

United States Office of Government and Ethics, (2014). The Hatch Act. Retrieved from the World Wide Web: http://www.oge.gov/Topics/Outside-Employment-and-Activities/Political-Activities/

About the Author

Having worked on political campaigns since 1993, Dr. Cristina Guarneri has provided seminars on Ethics and Leadership in Public Policy, her newest seminar Ethical Leadership in the 21st Century: The Issues in Public Policy has been held throughout the Tri-State area. Cristina has spoken on national radio for the last two years, speaking in the top 30 radio market.

Dr. Guarneri holds a doctorate in Leadership, Management, and Policy with a concentration in Public Policy from Seton Hall University, South Orange, NJ, and a professional certification in Public Performance Measurement: Government Affairs from Rutgers University, Newark, NJ. Dr. Guarneri writes a column on various topics concerning government and politics and is the author of the books *Twitterocracy* and *Twitterocracy: Social Media and Democracy*.